Quotation
From
Captain Paul Watson

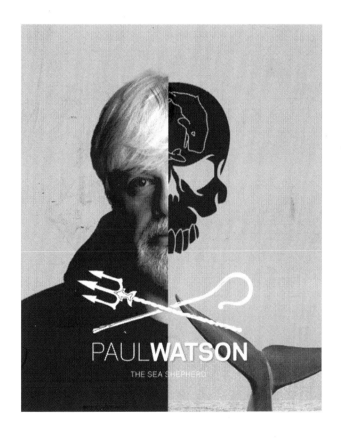

Inspiring Words
from an
Official Pirate
&
Modern Day Captain Nemo

Cover Art: Albian Gagica

Art by Sophie Cape

I have no concerns for the media spins
At the lies and falsehoods they scatter.
May the future forgive my ecological sins
For all other sins don't matter.

Captain Paul Watson

Captain Paul Watson

Captain Paul Watson was born on December 2nd, 1950 and raised in an Eastern Canadian fishing village called St. Andrew's-By-The-Sea.

He began his life of activism at the age of eleven by freeing animals from trap-lines and destroying leg-hold traps and snares.

At the age of 18 he was the youngest founding member of the Greenpeace Foundation.

He majored in communications at Simon Fraser University.

He worked as an Able Seaman in the Norwegian and Swedish merchant marine and served in the Canadian Coast Guard.

He began professional writing as a journalist for the Vancouver weekly underground newspaper, the Georgia Straight contributing from 1969 to the present day.

He served as a medic for the American Indian Movement during the occupation of Wounded Knee in 1973.

He founded the Sea Shepherd Conservation Society in 1977 and founded Friends of the Wolf in 1984. He was a national director of the Sierra Club 2003-2006.

He was officially labeled a pirate by the U.S. 9th Circuit Federal Court judge Alex Kozinski in 2012 although never charged with piracy.

He co-founded the Mars Conservation Society and the Church of Biocentrism in 2018.

His books include Ocean Warrior, Seal Wars, Cry Wolf!, Earthforce!, Sea Shepherd and The War That Saved The Whales.

Captain Watson is married to Yana Rusinovich Watson. He is the father to his daughter Lilliolani and his son Tiger.

Anthropocentrism
Biocentrism

"I view myself as a Bio centrist. I see humanity as just a small part of the global biosphere. We are not superior, nor are we dominant. We are not the most important species on the planet. In fact, there are far more important species than us. Most other species don't need us, but we need a great many other species to survive. In short we are not the whole but rather we are a small part of the whole."

"Anthropocentrism is the philosophical point of view that has led humanity to be alienated from the biocentric diversity of life. It is the idea that all life, all existence revolves around the human species. It is a view that I totally reject."

"The first step to freedom is to transcend the anthropocentric reality."

"The major failing within the environmental movement is the failure to see the Earth as sacred
Almost all theological thought is anthropocentric, and I just cannot buy into the anthropocentric ideology. Basically, we're a bunch of ecologically ignorant conceited naked apes who have become divine legends in our own minds."

☠☠☠☠☠☠☠

☠☠☠☠☠☠☠

"Oil! The drug that sustains humanity's ecological madness. We are all addicted, and we will destroy the Earth and each other to get our fix and once it is gone, this insanity of humanity will be no more."

"We delude ourselves into believing we are above all other creatures when we in fact are not a single creature ourselves. All humans like all animals are a collection of living organisms living symbiotically with each other. There are thousands of species of bacteria living on and in us. They help digest our food, manufacture needed vitamins and they even trim our eyelashes. We need them to survive and they need us in an ancient partnership of interdependence."

"If we could see through the eyes of other creatures, we would realize how utterly silly and selfish we are."

"A tree does what a tree does. A fish does what a fish does and we humans do what we do which for the most part consists of entertaining ourselves at the expense of other species."

"When it comes to crimes against the planet and other species, we are all guilty. It is impossible to live in our modern civilized society without being a hypocrite. What we can do is control just how hypocritical we choose to be
Almost all human religions are anthropocentric, placing humans at the center of creation. This is insanely delusional, extremely conceited and just plain stupid."

Is there no limit to the collective ecological insanity of humanity?

☠☠☠☠☠☠☠

☠☠☠☠☠☠☠

For the last few thousand years we humanoid monkey creatures have been having one hell of a party at the expense of practically every other species on the planet. We don't treat many of them with respect or even mild consideration, even the ones that look like us, like for example, the chimps and the apes or even those with larger more complex brains like whales and dolphins. In fact, we give most other species very little thought even when we're eating them or using them to work for us. We tend to give them more thought when we're killing them for pleasure or simply because we don't like them."

"The death of anthropocentrism will be the rebirth of the natural world."

"We hominid monkeys on this spinning ball of mud absolutely love anything to do with a ball. We like to throw balls, catch balls, kick balls, hit balls or better yet we love to watch other monkey creatures like ourselves throw balls, catch balls, kick balls and hit balls. Nothing gets a primate species like us more excited than the image of some ball passing between two posts, being tossed into some hoop or smacked with a stick into some distant hole in the ground. I'm partial myself to knocking a little dimpled ball through the open mouth of some moving clown and past the little windmills. I guess that makes me a golfer, I mean it makes about as much sense as the bigger version except the smaller version is more amusing and does not waste as much land."

"The major failing within the environmental movement is the failure to see the Earth as sacred."
☠☠☠☠☠☠☠

☠☠☠☠☠☠☠

"There are tens of millions of species on this planet. They're all Earthlings. They're all equal. Well, some are actually more 'equal' than others like earthworms, trees, bees and fish. These are species far more valuable than people for the simple reason that they don't need us but we do need them."

"For the most part we, the hairless monkeys, well relatively hairless anyhow, give little thought to where we came from, who we are, or where we are going. We are content as long as there is something to eat and drink, something to buy, another monkey to copulate or play with, or we have enough of a variety of stimulants and entertainment devices and the opportunity to throw balls around together."

"We go through life believing that we are the pinnacle of creation, in fact some of us think there is even a big angry all-powerful monkey-god in the sky who created us in his own image. Others believe we came here on some intergalactic spaceship and were dumped off as some sort of extraterrestrial relocation project. A great many of us monkeys even believe that once we die, we move on to some exotic divine paradise created from some poets' imagination where we will be happy forever, unless of course we are bad monkeys, as judged by more powerful monkeys who consider themselves more superior, who then say we will spend eternity being tortured and abused by ugly mythical monkeys for not obeying the big monkey God in the sky."
"I reject the idea that humans are superior to other life forms---
Man is just an ape with an
overly developed sense of superiority."

☠☠☠☠☠☠☠

7

☠☠☠☠☠☠☠

*"It is a fascinating and marvelous creation – this spaceship
Earth. It is a home to tens of millions of diverse and unique
species of beings, all of us inter-related and inter-dependent – all
of us, despite bearing feathers, leaves, scales, fur, and skin – all
of us having one thing in common
– we are Earthlings."*

*"Marriage is a peculiar monkey ritual and institution that states
two monkeys, a male and a female, will be united until death do
they part or when one or both say they are tired of each other, or
one of them decides to entertain a more attractive monkey,
causing the other to throw a monkey fit to end the bonds between
them both. This is because marriage is sacred in the eyes of the
monkey god in the sky who does not seem to like two monkeys of
the same sex being in love with each other because, well, just
because! Lately he seems to be forgiving about the 'until death do
you part.' thing and in a few places, he is allowing the gay
marriage thing in places where non-gay monkeys are more
amenable to gay marriages. The dominant monkey rules dictate
that being in love must conform to a general set of rules dictated
by the not so moral majority of monkeys who wish to control the
bodies and desires of other monkeys. Male monkeys especially
like to control the bodies of female monkeys which most likely
stems from a deep resentment that all male monkeys are
biologically half female anyhow being that femaleness is the
original sex despite the Garden and apple tree myth because all
females are XX whereas all males are XY except in rare
exceptions when a YY occurs and that usually is not pleasant."*
☠☠☠☠☠☠☠

8

☠☠☠☠☠☠☠

"To many environmentalists, the talk of sacredness in nature is nothing more than meaningless rhetoric. The desecration of the sacred, if the sacred really is sacred, will always inspire gut anger and will in all cases provoke an active response."

"I reject the idea that humans are superior to other life forms--- Man is just an ape with an overly developed sense of superiority."

"To a biocentrist, a redwood is more sacred than a religious icon, a species of bird or butterfly is of more value than the crown jewels of a nation, and the survival of a species of cacti is more important than the survival of monuments to human conceit like the pyramids or the Taj Mahal."

"The water of the Earth is the blood of the planet and within its immensity can be found the molecules which once enlivened the cells of our ancestors of all species. The water you drink once coursed through the blood of the dinosaurs, or was drunk by Pre-Cambrian ferns, or was expelled in the urine of a mastodon. Water has utilized the lives of all living things as part of its circulatory system. All life contains water. Therefore, water is sacred."

"The air that we breathe has passed through countless living respiratory systems and thus has been chemically stabilized by plants and animals. Without the lives that have gone before, there would be no air to breathe. The life of the past has nurtured the atmosphere. Therefore, the air is sacred."

☠☠☠☠☠☠☠

"The soil beneath our feet contains the material reality of the ancestors of all species. Without the expended lives of the past, there would be little soil. For this reason, the soil itself is our collective ancestry and thus the soil is sacred."

"I take a biocentric view. I look at things from the point of view of the Earth and the laws of ecology as opposed to the anthropocentric point of view where everything revolves around humanity."

"People are beginning to realize that we need to live in accordance with the laws of ecology and if we don't, we're going to become extinct. We're not even the captains of Spaceship Earth. We're just the passengers, entertaining ourselves and wasting resources. The crew of Spaceship Earth are the phytoplankton, the microbes, the insects, the fish, the whales, the birds and the trees doing what they do to keep the life support system functioning. And the passengers are killing off the essential crew, one by one."

"I am presently sitting way out here in the middle of a vast ocean that exists as a thin layer of moisture on the outside of a relatively small round rock somewhere inside an outer remote spiral arm of the Milky Way galaxy. This little blue and white ball of spinning mud is orbiting an average yellow star and sharing the experience with a diversity of wondrous living fellow Earthling beings, including some eight billion silly little monkeys just like me."

"We can only avoid natures' laws for so long without consequence."

10

☠☠☠☠☠☠

"Water is the blood of the Earth. The rivers are the veins and the arteries removing waste and delivering nutrients. The water is cleansed in the marshes and estuaries and circulated by the heart of the solar system, the Sun. When a dam is placed on a river, it is like cutting off an artery, nutrients can't be delivered downstream and waste builds up behind it."

"Ecological activists represent the majority of humans, because we represent all those billions of people who have yet to be born over the next ten thousand plus year. In addition, we represent the billions of individuals of the tens of millions of fellow planetary species."

"We need a biocentric religion that understands the reality that humans are a part of everything and not masters over everything."

"I have hope that humanity will be cured of our collective ecological insanity and that we can adapt to living within the boundaries of the laws of ecology."

"I remain hopeful that humanity will soon begin to realize that there is no greater challenge than stopping the diminishment of biodiversity in the sea and on land. The consequences if we fail will fall upon all of us and all future generations."

"As a species humanity is collectively sociopathic, collectively narcissistic and peppered with a shitload of psychopaths and pathological liars."

☠☠☠☠☠☠

"Not only do we separate ourselves from all other species, we separate ourselves from each other by race, tribe, gender, customs, ideology and with colorful banners, flags and baseball caps."

"After 3.5 billion years of evolution, we are fooling ourselves if we think that we are the pinnacle of the evolutionary process. We as humans are what future hominids will view tomorrow, the same way we view Australopithecus today, and twenty million years from now whatever intelligent life will be dominant will view as just curious fossils."

"If we take care to do good in the present,
The future will take care of itself.
Past, present, and future.
Together as one....
The Continuum."

Greenpeace
Sea Shepherd

*"Greenpeace is the world's biggest feel good organization.
People join it to feel good, an automatic ticket to
ecological salvation."*

*"Steve Shallhorn of Greenpeace made a statement that very few
Japanese eat whale meat on a regular basis. "Our polls show that
most Japanese wouldn't touch it with a 10-foot chopstick.
Captain Paul Watson replied: "I'm sure they wouldn't touch it
with a 10-foot chopstick. They prefer 8-inch chopsticks."*

*What began as a small nonprofit society (Sea Shepherd) in British
Columbia, Canada is, forty-two years later a global movement."*

*"Greenpeace denies that I am a Greenpeace founder. They
describe me as just an early member. What is amusing, is that
none of the Greenpeace people today were there at the time and
most had not yet been born.
I think the film How To Change the World
has put an end to their ridiculous revisionism."*

*"I was dismissed from the Greenpeace Board of Directors in
1977 for saving the life of a seal. I had taken a seal club from a
seal who was about to bash a seal pup in the head and I tossed it
in the sea. Greenpeace accused me of theft and destruction of
property. I mistakenly assumed I was leading an expedition to
save the lives of seals."*

☠☠☠☠☠☠☠

"In 2015, I applied for the position of Executive Director of Greenpeace. I told them I was a co-founder of Greenpeace and would do the job for $1 a year. They interviewed me twice and finally said that I did not have the experience for the job. I told them I was not surprised because I never did get a degree in accounting or fund-raising from Harvard University."

"Back in 1979 at an early meeting of the Don't Make a Wave Committee, someone left the meeting and flashed a peace sign and said 'peace.'
Bill Darnell replied, 'make it a green peace."
And Bob Hunter said;
"That's a great name for the boat, the Greenpeace."

"Greenpeace today is a multinational feel good organization. People donate to feel like they are part of the solution and not part of the problem."

"Greenpeace lost all credibility the day Greenpeace Denmark director Jon Burgwald put on a seal fur vest and declared that he attended a modern fur fashion show and tweeted that he thought it was cool. He said it was time to move on and to promote "sustainable" seal fur products."

"We are Neptune's Navy"

☠☠☠☠☠☠☠

☠☠☠☠☠☠☠

"Greenpeace leader David McTaggart once told me that I was an embarrassment to Greenpeace for ramming the pirate whaler Sierra. I told him that I bloody hell hope so. I am exceedingly proud to be an embarrassment to Greenpeace."

"Our enemies can stop us as individuals, they can shut us down as an organization, but they cannot stop a movement."

"We're the Ladies of the Night of the marine conservation movement. People may agree with us in the dark of night but don't want to be seen with us in the daylight."

"Sea Shepherd is an interventionist movement, not a protest organization. Protest is very submissive – it's like saying, "please, please, please, don't kill the whales." Then they go and kill them anyway – nobody cares. The fact is, you gotta stop them – you're dealing with ruthless people, and you have to stop them. But you have to do it in a responsible way, which just means you don't physically hurt them."
– The Guardian Sept 21, 2010

"Our supporters and Advisory Board members include Sean Connery and Pierce Brosnan, Christian Bale and Richard Dean Anderson, William Shatner and Christophe Lambert and Martin Sheen. So how can we lose? We have two James Bonds, Batman and McGyver, Captain Kirk and the Highlander and we have a President of the United States."

"We do not protest. Protesting is fundamentally submissive. We are enforcers. We enforce the law."

15

☠☠☠☠☠☠☠

"To be effective we need to unite with the surfers, the divers, the boaters, the musicians, the actors, the scientists, the fashion designers, the artists, the lawyers, the builders, the business community and with law enforcement. Strength for Sea Shepherd lies in diversity."

"For those who have criticized me over the years for being arrogant, for being stubborn, for being egotistical, for being foolhardy, I can say without shame or hesitation – you were right. I was, and perhaps I still am all these things. In many ways, I had to be stubborn and persistent, a little ruthless and most importantly I had to be arrogant. I no longer need to be these things. I simply had to lay a foundation for Sea Shepherd and after doing so I have had the pleasure of watching something very exciting being built."

"After being accused of being an eco-terrorist by Greenpeace in 1986, I replied:
"What do you expect from the Avon ladies of the Environmental movement."
They were not happy"

"We have created something unique, a non-governmental organization that partners with governments to uphold international conservation law."

"Sea Shepherd is a coalition of international volunteers united by passion, imagination and courage. We go where others fear to go and do what many say cannot be done."

16

"Sea Shepherd has taken me around the world, from Pole to Pole, to remote islands and atolls. The things that I have experienced, the things that I have seen, both horrific and beautiful, the people I have met and worked with, the magnificent creatures I have been tasked to protect, all of this has given meaning to my life and bestowed a happiness on me that I am eternally grateful for."

*"I am not Sea Shepherd.
Sea Shepherd is not an organization. It's a global movement that I am proud to be a part of. They can take down an individual. They can take down an organization, but they can't destroy a movement."*

Whales

"I think that the time will soon come when the world will recognize the rights of the Cetacean Nations. These are far more ancient cultures than any human culture. These are highly intelligence, socially complex sentient unique and extraordinary beings. It is my position after years of observation and thought that the killing of a whale or dolphin is an act of murder. We have invaded their realms and we have slaughtered them mercilessly for centuries, treating them contemptuously and disrespectfully with an arrogance born out of the fact that we are land based hominids. I have fought for the rights and lives of cetaceans for four decades and every year has brought me to a closer understanding of just how heinous and horrific our crimes against the Cetacean Nations have been. The shame of this disgraceful history of slaughter guides my heart and has been the reason that I have devoted my life to obstructing, harassing, intervening and confronting their cruel and ruthless killers. The killing of any whale or dolphin by any person of any human culture anywhere on this planet is a crime and will be judged so by more enlightened future generations."

"In 1975, I looked into the eye of a dying whale and what I saw there changed my life forever. I saw understanding. The whale understood what I was trying to do. He could have killed me, but did not. I am alive today because that whale chose to not take my life."

"I find it abhorrent to see a whale being slaughtered and do nothing but bear witness and hang banners."

☠☠☠☠☠☠☠

"When we pull back the blue shroud of the sea and peer deep into the inky blackness of the mysterious world below, we cannot see, but we most certainly can hear the voice and the songs of the Cachalot."

"There is no other living thing on this planet that can compare with this giant of the depths. The largest, most complex and developed brain of any animal, an explorer of the deep ocean navigating at crushing depths guided by sonar and the ability to use sound as a weapon in its hunt for squid. The Cachalot is without a doubt, the greatest mind in the sea and in my opinion, the greatest and most beautiful mind to have ever existed on this planet."

"I saw the eye of the Cachalot. He saw me. He dove and I watched as a trail of bloody bubbles approached us rapidly until his head rose high out of the water, towering over us at an angle so that he merely had to drop upon us to crush us.
As he rose from the water a shower of brine and blood rained down upon us. His head rose up beside us, so close I could have encircled one of his teeth in his lower jaw with my fingers, I saw my reflection in his eye and I caught a glimmer of understanding.
I felt that the whale sensed what we had tried to do.
Instead of falling forward, the dying whale forced himself back as he began to sink into the sea, I saw his eye slide beneath the surface still looking straight at me until it disappeared into the darkening depths, and he was gone."

☠☠☠☠☠☠☠

"As the sun sank and the lights of the Soviet whaling fleet began to sparkle over the gray water, I asked myself why? Why were they killing these magnificent, beautiful, intelligent, self-aware, social complex sentient beings? No one hunted the Cachalot for food. They were killed for the highly prized spermaceti and sperm oil in their bodies. Why because it is an oil with high heat resistant properties and one of the most valued uses was for lubricating intense heat producing machinery and one of those purposes was to provide the lubrication for Intercontinental Ballistic Missiles
These wonderful beings were being killed for the purpose of manufacturing weapons meant for the mass extermination of human beings! That was the moment my entire perspective shifted with the realization that the human species, my species was clearly and murderously insane."

"Maybe whales don't actually migrate. Maybe it's the barnacles that migrate and the whales being good natured simply go along for the ride."

"Whales! These awesome and magnificent armless Buddha's, these mysterious minds in the sea have always been and will always be the soul of our oceans and I ca not and would not live in a world without them."

"I have never met a single human being who has seen a whale and remained untouched by what they have experienced."

"Whales are the farmers of the Ocean, fertilizing the planets' essential crops of phytoplankton."

☠☠☠☠☠☠☠

"It always fascinates me when my crew rush to the bow in excitement to watch whales or dolphins. Their exclamations, excitement and sheer pleasure at observing these amazing creatures elicits a response that I can only describe as a 'dolphasm'".

"I do not pay much attention to criticism from people. My clients are the whales and I speak for them with no need for apologies for their killers or those who defend their killers".

"To me the killing of a whale or dolphin is an act of murder."

"I am opposed to the killing of any whale or dolphin by any person, anywhere for any reason. The murder of cetaceans has no economic, political or cultural justification."

"In Biology 101, my teacher posted pictures of the brains of a mouse, a dog, a chimp and a human. She pointed out how the brain of each was larger than the next and that the convulsions on the neo-cortex were more pronounced and complex than the next. I asked her why she did not show us a brain of an Orca or a Sperm whale and suggested that perhaps it was because it would make us look really stupid."

"Dolphins are more intelligent than humans, they have larger more complex brains. They are very social, and they have communication abilities far superior than people."

"I have seen my reflection in the eye of a whale and what I saw was both enemy and friend."

"The human brain is 1700 cubic centimeters. The Orca has a 6000-cubic centimeter brain, and the Sperm whale has the largest brain ever evolved at 9000 cubic centimeters. All mammals have three lobed brains except cetacean which have four lobed brains. Much more complex.
No Orca has ever attacked a human being in the wild, yet Tilikum, a captive whale killed three people. The answer is that captivity causes psychotic insanity in Orcas."

"Back in 1980, whale watching surpassed whaling as an industry. Now it's worth about four times as much. Whale watching provides far more jobs to people than whaling ever did. Whale watching has become an ally in the fight to end whaling."

"Every day a Blue whale defecates some 3 tons of whale shit into the sea and that manure is rich with iron and nitrogen, the essential nutrients for phytoplankton. Since 1950 we have seen a 40% diminishment of phytoplankton populations because of the diminishment of whales, dolphins and sea birds. Fewer whales means less phytoplankton and if phytoplankton disappears – so do we!"

"We really should change the names of some whale species. The Right whale gets it's name from the fact it was the right whale to kill. I would call it Payne's whale after Dr.Roger Payne. I would rename the Minke whale as the Piked Whale, no whale should be named after a whale killer."

22

☠☠☠☠☠☠☠

"In 1975 in the Bella Bella Straits, we saw a pod of Orcas approaching. Three of us jumped into the sea ahead of them. Now to see an oncoming pod of Orcas from the deck of a boat is quite different than seeing them approaching in the water. I thought to myself that these guys eat sea lions and sea lions are bigger than us. Now the only thing scarier than an oncoming pod of Orcas is when they dive and disappear but when they surfaced alongside of us, I reached out and grabbed the dorsal of one of them and suddenly I was pulled along. I was riding a whale for about 200 meters until I fell off and watched them swim away. It was awesome."

"Whales are hunted with both harpoons and cameras and in some cases the camera has become as lethal as the harpoon. It's called irresponsible whale watching."

"The only good whaling ship is a sunken whaling ship."

"We sank half of Iceland's whaling fleet in 1986."

"The slaughter of the whales is one of the greatest crimes by humanity:

"Moby Dick was my favorite hero."

"The crew of the Essex got exactly what they deserved."

"The one good thing the Confederate Navy did was to destroy the Yankee whaling fleet."

☠☠☠☠☠☠☠

Whale Wars

"Attention all crew, stand by to ram."

"People sometimes feel frustrated about what's going on in our oceans and environment, and 'Whale Wars' shows that ordinary people can take action and make things happen."

"It is true that many of the Sea Shepherd crewmembers are inexperienced, but the fact is that these volunteers bring a passion to the project that cannot be found in a hired crew."

"In 'Deadliest Catch,' we have men in ships in rough cold seas doing dangerous things in a very remote area for the purpose of catching crabs. I said to Animal Planet that I could give them men and women from many nations working in a colder, much rougher and more remote ocean doing something far more dangerous for the purpose of saving whales. Plus, we could throw in some penguins, orcas and icebergs. That's how I sold them on Whale Wars."

"Animal planet did not tell us what to do or where to go and we did not tell them what to shoot or how to edit the show. We did not have a script. We did what we did as if they were not there and they followed with their cameras

"I did have two types of volunteer crewmembers. Those who wanted to save whales and those who wanted to be on television. Fortunately, the latter were the minority because quite frankly they were a pain in the ass."

24

"The real war on the show was between the producers and the Sea Shepherd officers. The producers wanted to create interpersonal dramas and we refused. They wanted the same type of personalities that were shown in Deadliest Catch. I told them we were very different than the crab fishermen and they were not going to find any drug addicts, wife beaters, alcoholics or psychos on my crew"

"I did have two types of volunteer crewmembers. Those who wanted to save whales and those who wanted to be on television. Fortunately, the latter were the minority because quite frankly they were a pain in the ass."

"I have to say that helicopter pilot Chris Aultman was the greatest asset for producing Whale Wars. The producer thought so also, so much so that she married him."

"I think that Whale Wars was the best unscripted reality show ever produced. It was the flagship program on Animal Planet for years and won rave reviews."

"In the end Animal Planet was intimidated by the Japanese government and put an end to the Whale Wars series. On the positive side we got what we want – global awareness of Japanese crimes in the Southern Ocean."

Antarctica

"I believe that I have led more expeditions (8) to Antarctica than Scott, Amundsen, and Shackleton put together."

"Of all the places I've been, the seas I've crossed, the mountains I've climbed, there is no other place on this planet that I have seen and experienced that is so stunningly beautiful, so wildly and spectacularly magnificent, so profoundly awesome – as Antarctica!"

"The Steve Irwin under my command set the record for the furthest point of navigation on the planet in 2011 in the Bay of Whales on the Hundredth Anniversary of Amundsen's departure for the pole, from the very same bay."

"I stood on the edge of the Ross Ice Shelf, a hundred feet above the sea. Two hundred miles of ice on either side and 500 miles of ice behind me, and before me thousands of miles of Ocean, unobstructed by land, all the way to the North Pole. It was like standing on the threshold of the entire planet and it was magically, amazingly, magnificent."

"Every year my crew and I took the opportunity to swim nude with the penguins. It was quite invigorating and a little crazy."

"We brought some ice back from an iceberg and it was used for making what became the most expensive bottle of beer in brewing history. I auctioned off one bottle of Antarctic Nail Ice for $1500 in Fremantle, Western Australia and a 2nd bottle for $2500 in Sydney, New South Wales."

☠☠☠☠☠☠☠

"Roland Huntford is a cold and timid soul, and his praise for Roald Amundsen is shallow. Huntford is an armchair explorer and exploits Amundsen to humble Scott.
As Scott wrote in one of his letters; "What lots and lots I could tell you of this journey. How much better has it been than lounging in too great comfort at home…"
Scott was a doer of deeds not a critic of others."
Letter to Encounter Magazine. May 1980

"The vastness, the whiteness, the coldness, the remoteness, the solitude, the quiet and the peacefulness.
These are the reasons I love Antarctica."

"Yes, it takes skill and courage to navigate through pack ice but it also takes something more and that something is an intuitive understanding of the nature of ice."

Animals and Plants

We are all animals

"My greatest teachers have been animals."

"To most animals, all human beings are Nazis."

"If you want to know where you would have stood on slavery before the Civil War, don't look at where you stand on slavery today. Look at where you stand on animal rights now."

"I define intelligence as the ability to live in harmony with the environment and by that criteria, all animals and plants are intelligent – humans not so much."

"All Animals need plants to live and many plants need animals to procreate. Plants and animals evolved together. Sometimes animals manipulate plants and at other times plants manipulate animals. This is true of humans also. We manipulate plants for our own purposes, yet these same plants manipulate humanity to serve their own purpose."

When people ask how can I justify eating plants? The simple answer is we evolved to eat plants and plants need us and other animals because for many plants we are part of their sex life. Some plants need animals to spread their seed and to pollinize. We serve the plants and they serve us and that translates into equality between plants and animals."

"Plants fascinate me. They eat sunshine and feed every animal on the planet directly or indirectly."

28

☠☠☠☠☠☠☠

"Inside every apple there is a star and inside every star is a future apple."

"The Planet has two lungs, one blue and the other green."

"A tree is our brother; a flower is our sister."

"To speak the language of flowers is to realize absolute happiness and contentment."

"Monsanto is to plants what cancer is to humans."

"The trees are patiently waiting to reclaim the world and to flourish once we are gone."

"Unlike animals, plant have evolved to be eaten. For many plants, it's simply part of their reproduction process."

Elephants

"To slaughter such grand and beautiful creatures like these tuskers, solely to obtain their teeth indicates that we have not evolved very much since the days our forebears lived in caves and sought to prove their superiority by adorning themselves with bones, teeth and claws."

"I spent three months helping to track elephant poachers in Kenya (1978) to gather evidence for a U.S. Congressional Bill to ban ivory. It was a dangerous, frustrating, heartbreaking campaign."

"I was a little worried that our visas (Jet Johnson and I) from the Ugandan mission were numbered 001 and 002".

"Jet and I were denied entry into Uganda because Idi Amin had a premonition that two CIA agents were coming to assassinate him. Actually, although we were not CIA agents, we did actually talk about shooting the bastard. When I asked Jet how he would escape, he laughed and said, "Escape, there will be no escape, but it would save the lives of lots of elephants and people."

"Seeing elephants in the wild is a truly magnificent experience."

"Historians have often been puzzled as to how Hannibal was able to tame African elephants. Most experts agree that African elephants are not tamable. The answer is that Hannibal did not use African elephants. He used European elephants, a sub-species from Northern Africa that are now quite extinct. We destroy and forget."

30

Seals & Sealers

"The seal hunt makes me ashamed to be a Canadian."

"If you want more fish, you need more seals. The biggest predators of cod are the fish that harp and hood seals eat. Diminish seal populations and you diminish the cod."

"500 years ago, there were some 45 million seals in the North Atlantic. There was no shortage of fish."

*"I have seen seal pups kicked in the face.
I've seen them skinned alive.
Canadian sealers are exceptionally cruel barbarians."*

"Seals are to dogs what mermaids are to humans."

*"When Bob Hunter and I stood on that ice floe in the path of that Norwegian sealing ship, with the ice breaking up under our feet, Bob said to me, "I'm not moving."
I replied, "Damn, I guess I won't be moving either."
After years of effort we finally achieved a ban on seal products by the European Parliament. It was a great victory."*

*"The missionaries used the baby harp seal to convey the meaning of the 'Lamb of God" to the Inuit.
The Canadian government propaganda is that opposition to the slaughter of seals is opposition to Inuit culture and thus racist, yet no one has ever physically opposed the Inuit seal hunt of some 10,000 adult seals each year."*

"There is no difference between a Canadian sealer and a Columbian cocaine farmer except that the Columbian cocaine farmer actually needs the money."

☠☠☠☠☠☠☠

"The sealers of the Magdalen Islands sent me a T-shirt saying 'Phoque you Paul Watson.' They also sent me a petition with 5,000 names of Magadalen Islanders saying 'Phoque you.' I was very flattered. I love that shirt.

"Killing a baby seal is about the easiest thing you can do if you're inclined to be sadistic; you certainly can't say there's any sport in it - the animal is totally defenseless".

"The centuries of mass slaughter of tens of millions of harp seals is one of the greatest crimes by humanity against the natural world."

"I was amazed to see the images of our fight against the Canadian seal slaughter, Faeroese pilot whale killing, the dolphin slaughter in Japan, and illegal Japanese whaling all presented in a positive light on Canadian television. There were certainly a few disgruntled baby seal bashers drowning their anger in their beer that evening, I'm sure, saying nasty things about me not realizing that I enjoy hearing that the sealers are saying nasty things about me. I'm not their friend. I don't want to be their friend. They know it and I know it and they know that it is my ultimate objective to wipe out their abominable industry."
So, I'm happy the show pissed them off.
Commenting on CTV's W5 episode: Watson's War

"In 1976, I wrote an article about leading the Greenpeace seal campaign that year. The title of the article was Shepherds of the Labrador Front. This was the inspiration for the name of the Sea Shepherd ship and the Sea Shepherd Conservation Society."

Big Game Hunters

"I think that anyone who feels the need to kill a magnificent animal in order to mount its head and hang it on the wall suffers from a serious sexual and psychological disorder."

"You don't love nature with a gun."

"What we need are big game hunters that will specialize in hunting big game hunters."

"I have to confess that I am a fan of hunting accidents. I also enjoy a good bullfight but only if the bull wins."

"Big game fishermen are just as cruel and destructive as those who murder animals on land. There is no difference in my eyes between a Big Game Hunter and a Big Game Fisherman."

"In the movie the PREDATOR we saw an alien big game trophy hunter hunting humans. He had rules – only armed humans, no pregnant humans, no children. I wonder, would they let him join Safari Club International."

"I have to confess; I do love hunting accidents."

"You can't call hunting a sport. One side has all the advantages and only one side dies. One side is minding their own business and the other side are psychopathic killers forcing their perversion on innocent victims."

Fish and Fishermen

"A fish is more valuable swimming in the sea maintaining the integrity of oceanic eco-systems than it is on anyone's plate."

"Sustainable fishing is a fraud. It's a marketing term that really means business as usual."

"There is no such thing as sustainable fishing. It's a myth."

"Fish are sentient.
They feel pain, they think. They're self-aware."
"Seafood is simply a socially acceptable form of bush meat. We condemn Africans for hunting monkeys and mammalian and bird species from the jungle, yet the developed world thinks nothing of hauling in magnificent wild creatures like swordfish, tuna, halibut, shark, and salmon for our meals. The fact is that the global slaughter of marine wildlife is simply the largest massacre of wildlife on the planet."
"We are literally eating the Ocean alive and there are simply not enough fish to continue to feed an ever-expanding population of humanity."
"Bluefin tuna are the cheetahs of the sea. It's the fastest aquatic predator. It's warm blooded and with a $100,000 price tag on its head it is becoming quite rare."
"Every day enough long lines, drift nets and gill nets are set that would circle the globe."

☠☠☠☠☠☠☠

☠☠☠☠☠☠☠

*"The Polynesians used to have a system where they proclaimed a fishing area as 'kapu.' If any fisherman was caught fishing in a kapu area, they would be killed.
The Polynesians understand that their survival depended upon the survival of the fish."*

"For fish, there are no safe places."

"On the Santa Monica pier, there are signs in English, Spanish and Vietnamese saying that it is not healthy to eat any fish caught from the pier. Yet every day there are a few dozen guys fishing with poles. It's a Darwinian observation."

"I was raised in a fishing village and I'll be blunt, I don't like commercial fishermen. They are mass murdering, polluting, selfish, anthropocentric scum and they may well be the reason for the collapse of marine eco-systems and thus human civilization."

"Politicians tend to be afraid of fishermen and fishermen tend to get what they want. I attribute this to a thing I call homopecheaphobia – politicians and their fear of fishermen."

"A fish is more valuable swimming in the sea, maintaining the integrity of oceanic eco-systems than it is on anyone's plate."

*"Fishermen could bring an end to civilization. If the fish are diminished, the sea is diminished and if the sea is diminished, humanity is diminished.
If the sea dies, we all die!"*

☠☠☠☠☠☠☠

*"I have spent a great deal of time underwater with the fishes and I see them as self-aware sentient beings that belong in a world that we humans have invaded.
The sea is their home and we are the homewreckers."*

"When I was five my father kept catching trout and tossing them on the bank. When he finished fishing, he had dozens of dead fish lying on the ground. He picked up the largest four and left the others behind. I despised him for that."

"There is no massacre anywhere on earth to compare with the massacre of fish. People pay little attention to their suffering and that is reflected in the language that we use when we talk about "stocks" and "tons." We have such little regard for them that people who claim to be vegetarians continue to eat fish without thinking it is in the least bit contradictory."

"I've swum with piranhas in the Amazon, done night dives with salmon in Alaska, shared my lunch with catfish in Vermont, hiked along the bottom of the sea with an octopus, freed lobster from cages in Maine, freed bluefin tuna from nets off Libya, and had numerous adventures with fish around the world. So, when people ask me how do I like my fish, my answer is that I like to have them as friends."

I was at a Conservation International event in the Dominican Republic with Sylvia Earle. We went to lunch where we saw this tremendous smorgasbord of seafood. We were stunned. This was an event to discuss saving fish. Sylvia said to me, 'we've along way to go yet.'

Sharks

*"The shark is the apex predator in the sea. Sharks have molded
evolution for 450 million years.
All fish species that are prey to the sharks have had their
behavior, their speed, their camouflage and
their defense mechanisms molded by the shark."*

*"It's safer to play golf than to swim with sharks. More people die
on golf courses every year from lightning strikes and bee stings
than are killed by sharks."*

*"My advice to any surfer, diver or swimmer afraid of sharks is
simple. Stay the hell out of the water!"*

*"I have always felt safer swimming with sharks than with walking
down the streets of a major city. From experience, I trust sharks
more than people."*

*"On average seven humans are killed every year by sharks.
Humans on the other hand slaughter 75 million sharks each year
primarily for the fins to make a non-nutritional soup. It seems to
me that the monster here is not the shark."*

The Vaquita

"If not for our Operation Milagro over the past four years, the Vaquita would now be extinct."

"We have seized over 100,000 meters of illegal gills nets in the Vaquita Refuge, which is higher than Mount Everest and deeper than the Marianas Trench."

"We have sent five ships into the Sea of Cortez along with hundreds of volunteers. We are committed to saving the Vaquita from extinction and as long as there is a living female and a living male, we will continue our patrols."

"The poachers shot down one of our drones on Christmas Eve. (2017) They are getting desperate it seems. We need to be more careful, but we will not be intimidated."

"I have been told repeatedly that our campaign to save the Vaquita is a lost cause. I love lost causes; they are the most challenging and most rewarding causes to fight for."

"I warned the Vaquita CPR people they would kill a Vaquita. They refused to even discuss the possibility with me. They killed a Vaquita at a cost of six million dollars."

"I never dreamt that marine conservation work would make us the enemies of the Mexican drug cartels. But when the swim bladder of the totoaba fish is worth more in weight than cocaine, it was inevitable.

Children

"I feel that people should have a license to have children, that a guarantee must be made that they have a proper education on how to raise children. Nobody should be allowed to be a parent unless they can prove that they are competent and responsible enough to be a parent."

"When you father or mother a child, you are obligated within the Continuum to bear responsibility for the protection, nourishment, nurturing, and education of the child. To not do so is the greatest irresponsibility and one of the gravest crimes a human can commit."

"With the birth of a child, the parents set in motion a series of events which will ripple forward into the future of the Earth. With the birth of one, you bring forth thousands. The psychology of one generation deeply affects the psychology of the next and so on."

"As long as the unborn is physically attached to the mother, the child and the mother are one and the same. The child is not an individual if it cannot sustain itself. The woman as mistress of her own body, has every right to judge and decide on the welfare and future of her body, mind and soul."

"Children have a natural intuitive knowledge that is gradually lost as they get older."

"I have observed how our education system takes bright, inquisitive, intelligent children and transforms them."

☠☠☠☠☠☠☠

"When anthropocentric society dictates that the law of the state overrules the freedom of the individual to decide her own fate and chart her own course, such legislation amounts to rape of the individual woman
by the brutish might of the faceless state."

"By outlawing pre-natal abortion, the state brings into being the practice of post-natal abortion and thus a child is set on the road of life burdened with the emotional scars of being unloved, uncared for and abused."

"When people ask me what shall we teach our children, my first response is to ask them what do they think their children can teach them?"

"My daughter, my son, my granddaughter and my grandson are my gifts of hope to the future."

"When my critics tell me to grow up,
all I can say is why? There's no joy in that."

"Children have an intuitive awareness of the laws of nature, of ethics and of compassion. We should never try to discourage such intuition. Instead we need to encourage them to learn and to express their thoughts, their emotions and their intuitive points of view. Children have the ability to see what adults once saw and many have since forgotten. They know that animals are not objects, that the Earth and the Ocean must be protected, and that life, all life, is precious. We do not need to simply prepare our children for the future, we need to listen to them and to embraces their perspectives, their vision and their passion for nature and for life."

☠☠☠☠☠☠☠

"I asked an Alaskan fisherman to think of the future, if for nothing else that his children would have fish and wild animals in their future. He looked at me and said, "In five years my mortgage will be paid and after that I could not give a damn. Now why does someone like that have children? It seems that it's because that's what you do."

"I would never beat my child; the very thought is repugnant. I was beaten severely as a child and all that it accomplished was to beat any love that I had for my father out of me. I never hated him for it, but I also did not love him. The strap simply made me indifferent to him."

"Children are not the property of their parents."

"Children are not born racist; they are not born to be cruel. These things are taught. Children are born to be curious. They are born to be kind. Upon the foundation of innocence our society through our schools and media constructs the twin towers of racism and cruelty."

Climate Change

"We are all involved, we are all responsible."

"As Voltaire so eloquently put it; "no snowflake in an avalanche ever feels responsible."

"Winter is coming and it's going to be very warm."

"The Ocean is the primary life support system for the planet. The phytoplankton within produces the oxygen we breathe, it provides food, it cleans and recycles our water and it regulates climate."

"I attended COP 21 in Paris. It was the biggest damn political ego-fest photo op bullshit useless festival that I've ever seen and that was about it."

"The slaughter of 65 billion animals a year creates more greenhouse gases than the entire transportation industry."

"We could be doomed because of a diminishment of whale shit and an excess of cow farts."

"How do you even begin to have an intelligent discussion with people who believe hurricanes are caused by gay marriage. Anyone who denies that climate change is a threat is a moron but unfortunately the world is governed by a great many morons."

"Humanity has an incredible ability for denial even in the face of imminent destruction."

☠☠☠☠☠☠☠

"Ignoring climate change as a reality will bring down nature's wrath with deadly fury. We shall see deadly storms, floods, fires, ecological refugees, famine, pestilence and social discord unlike anything humanity has ever experienced."

"Stronger storms, rising sea levels, floods, devastating record forest fires, disappearing species, radical changes in eco-systems, retreating glaciers, collapsing Antarctic ice shelves, crop failures, the emergence of new viruses and parasites, and yet the climate change deniers continue to demand proof."

"Politicians know they can't sit around and do nothing about climate change so what they do is hold meetings and conferences where they can sit around and talk about how they intend to do something about climate change."

"The one thing that climate change denying politicians like Donald Trump and climate change acceptance politicians like Justin Trudeau have in common is they are both equally doing nothing to address the problem."

"Climate change deniers don't understand that denying climate change will not negate the reality of climate change. They may as well deny gravity
Before anything is ever done about it, mankind will have to feel the full brunt of global warming."

"We can adapt to climate change the easy way
or the hard way, but knowing human nature,
my bet is we will choose the hard way."

☠☠☠☠☠☠☠

"Humanity will have to choose between consumerism and survival, and it appears that humanity believes their cars ,iPhones, televisions, steaks and luxuries are more valuable than survival."

"Climate change denying Donald Trump is the Piped Piper of America. Where he leads the ignorant will follow in search of things they don't need or understand. "

"You don't need a climatologist to know The degree where ice melts."

"Climate change is the key that will unlock the prison within the permafrost that will release an extinction level threat from pathogens that have been imprisoned for tens of thousands of years."

"Climate change is triggering zoonotic transmission of viruses from diminished eco-systems and other species to humanity. As other species disappear the viruses associated with them will look for new hosts and eight billion humans represent a very attractive new herd of hosts."

Confrontations

"I love confrontations at sea, especially confrontations with ships. Such situations are exciting and invigorating, allowing decisions to be guided by experience and instinct.
There is no time for doubt, for fear or hesitation.
Decisions are made instantaneously and
time seems to be slower as clarity is enhanced."

"When I had some bureaucrat from the Canadian Navy accuse us of not knowing what we are doing I just pointed out that we had rammed more ships, sunk more ships, boarded more ships and blockaded more harbors than the Canadian Navy has done since World War II."

"We fired pie filling. That was in the Faroe Islands in 1986. When they tried to board us, we hit them with forty-five-gallon shots of custard and banana cream pie."

"Confrontations must be accompanied by education, what Miyamoto Musashi once described as the twofold way of pen and sword and what I have described as the two-fold way of camera and sword."

"I have always held two rules to be my guide. The first is to never cause a physical injury to my opponent and the second is to always abide by the laws of ecology."

"I have always had this feeling that I can't explain, that my actions will not cause any injury or deaths and for forty years our actions have not caused a single death or injury."

"Spiking trees is the inoculation of a forest against a disease called clear-cutting."

☠☠☠☠☠☠☠

"All confrontation is based on deception."

"I am a biocentric ocean conservation activist. My clients are marine mammals, sea turtles, seabirds, fish, plankton etc. I represent their interests. I am not a people person. I am not politically correct. I thoroughly detest whalers, sealers, poachers, blood sport advocates, trophy hunters, animal abusers, clear cut loggers, palm oil farmers, rainforest burners, child abusers and a whole lot of other despicable forms of behavior. I oppose the killing of whales and dolphins by anyone, anywhere at any time for any reason and I am not interested in rationalizations or cultural justifications. I prefer to be ecologically correct. I say things some people don't like to hear. I do things that some people don't like me doing. I rock the boat, hell I have sunk a few boats sometimes. I piss some people off.
I offend others, because when I go on the offensive, my intention is to offend."

Crew

"My crew may be inexperienced, and they may be amateurs, but the truth is that I could not pay professionals to do what my crew do for nothing. It is the passion and the courage of our crews that makes our campaigns successful."

"Without volunteers, my crew on my ships and the volunteers on shore, I should think we would accomplish very little."

"The perfect crew is what you get when you weed out the whiners, the wimps, the weirdos and the mattress lovers."

"On the whole, women make better volunteer crewmembers than men. They whine less, show off less, boast less, compete less and work harder."

"If they want to call us pirates, well, we shall be pirates, jolly roger and all, but with a difference in that we are gentle and compassionate pirates."

*"You can never be faulted for who you hire but you can certainly be faulted for who you don't fire.
(John Paul DeJoria said this to me.)"*

"When someone wishes to join my crew, I asked them if they are willing to risk their life to defend a whale. If they say no, they are rejected. Some critics have said this is asking to much. I disagree. We ask young people to risk their lives to defend real estate, oil wells, flags and religion. I think risking your life to defend an endangered species or habitat is a far nobler cause."

Culture

The root of the word 'culture' is 'cult'.

Any 'culture" that enshrines and glorifies suffering and death has no place in the 21st Century.

The Kayapo people of Amazonia call us the 'termite people' because we gobble up all that lives.

We suffer in prison cells that we ourselves have constructed and our luxuries and entertainments are the locks that keep us incarcerated.

The Latin word for death is 'mort' and thus the word mortgage means a 'contract onto death.

Racism is illogical. There is only one race – the human race.

The only significant culture is the culture to be found in a petri dish.

Eco-Terrorism

*"Sea Shepherd is to terrorism
what Groucho was to Marxism."*

*"This is the contradiction we have in the media. We love
vigilantes: Batman, Tarzan, Green Arrow – the comic books and
the TV shows are filled with vigilantes. We love to promote it.
Jesus Christ was a vigilante. We admire such people, but we
don't want to be associated with them."*

"I'm not interested in culture; I'm interested in the law."

"Ecoterrorism is terrorism against the environment".

*"The Interpol Red List is for serial killers, war criminals and
major drug traffickers. I am the only person in the history of
Interpol to be placed on that list for conspiracy
to trespass on a whaling ship."*

*"To me extremism is targeting endangered whales in a whale
sanctuary in violation of a moratorium.
That, to me, is extreme."*

*"I'm not an eco-terrorist. I've never worked for Monsanto.
Put me on the blue list, the red list, the blacklist, the death list, the
anything but the 'I don't give a damn' list."*

*"We cannot commit an act of violence against a non-sentient
object. Violence can only be inflicted upon a living thing."*

"I was doing a radio talk show in Vancouver and somebody called in a bomb threat to protest my violence, which I thought was quite bizarre. We had to evacuate the building.
After evacuating the building after the bomb threat, a reporter pushed a microphone at my face and shouted, "Greenpeace has just condemned you as an 'eco-terrorist.' What is your response? Now I did not want to get into a big argument over Greenpeace, so I replied, Well, what do you expect from the Avon ladies of the environmental movement? They've never forgiven me for that"

"To the Green Party of Canada in 1986: You condemn our sinking of two whaling ships as violent, yet this Party proudly supports abortion. I am not anti-abortion, but the fact is that it is a violent act against life, so how is it that you condemn the destruction of some floating piece of metal yet condone the violent termination of a foetus. The response was that they support a woman's right to choose. I replied, so do I, but I also support the right of a whale to live."

Eco-Warriors

"If the Ocean Dies, we all die!"

"Protesting is fundamentally submissive. It's just, "please, pretty please, don't kill the whales."

"Sometimes going to jail is just the price you have to pay for social reform or social change."

"I always try to take the unexpected things and make them work for me."

"All strategy is based on deception."

"Environmental activists may be a nuisance and a pain in the ass to the established authorities of the present. However, to the establishment of the future, we will be honored ancestors."

"Remember always that it is the nature of a warrior to act. Do not be daunted by the formidable strength of the opposition. Do not be depressed by doom and gloom predictions. A true warrior must welcome challenge and must always seek to transform the impossible into the possible."

"Do not concern yourself with what others might think of you. The strategy of an eco-warrior activist is to say unpopular things that piss people off, to undertake actions which anger and disturb some people, and to boldly strike at issues and ideologies none have dared to strike at before."

"What is truly terrifying to my enemies are my ideas, not my actions,"

Extinction

"We'll lose more species of plants and animals between 2000 and 2065 than we've lost in the last 65 million years. If we don't find answers to these problems, we're going to be victims of this extinction event that we're at fault for."

"This is the sixth major planetary extinction event. The Earth has recovered from five previous extinction events. The Permian extinction 250 million years ago wiped out 97% of all living things and what I have learned is that it takes some 18 to 20 million years to recover from a planetary extinction event – so, in 20 million years, this will be a beautiful teeming with life and diversity planet once again."

"If humanity wipes itself out because of our ecological stupidity there will be one positive result. It will make this planet magnificent again."

"I am bothered greatly that we have driven so many animals and plants into extinction over the last few centuries and even worse that we have forgotten that many of them ever existed. Gone are the Labrador duck, the Newfoundland and Great Plains wolf, the Eastern Bison, the European Tiger and European elephant, the Carolina Parakeet, the Giant Auk, the Atlantic Grey whale, the Sea Mink, the Tasmanian Tiger, and so many more. Gone and forgotten because of the arrogance and greed of our own species."

"Specicide the deliberate causing of the extinction of a species is the greatest crime that humanity can commit."

☠☠☠☠☠☠☠

"Compared with a world in ecological collapse, all the wars, famines and epidemics that have marked the history of the planet will look like a picnic. Everything that our human civilizations have accomplished, everything that we have built, all the stories we have told and the songs and poems that we have written will be lost and forgotten."

"The Triassic Jurassic, the Permian, the late Devonian, the Ordovician and the Cambrian are the five major mass extinction events in this planet's history. We are now in the sixth major extinction event and it is stamped with our name – the Anthropocene."

"Our Flag, our own Jolly Roger symbolized our war against extinction. The black represents extinction. The skull represents humanity as the cause. The shepherd's staff represents our defense of life in the sea and the trident represents what we do – aggressive non-violence. The yin yang of the dolphin and the whale represents the mind in the sea and the harmony that is the interconnectedness of all life in the ocean."

First Nations

"My 12th Great Grandfather was Chief Henri Membertou, of the Mi'kmak in Acadia (1490-1560), the father of Chief Henricus Kjisaqmaw, Shaman of the Mi'maq (1507-1611, who was father to Catherine LeJeune (1633-1672) my 9th Great Grandmother. My roots go back over 500 years in Acadia and with the Mi'kmak. I have a heritage that I am deeply honored to possess."

"One of the most important lessons in my life was when I was in Wounded Knee in March 1973 during the occupation of Wounded Knee by the American Indian Movement. We were surrounded and heavily outnumbered by Federal agents and troops. I said to Russell Means that I did not think we could possibly win. He said to me, "we are not concerned with winning or losing nor are we concerned about the odds against us. We're here because it is the right thing to do and the right place to be."
That is a lesson that has guided me throughout my entire life."

"There are dozens of monuments and museums dedicated to the Jewish Holocaust but none for the genocide of the indigenous people of the Americas. Monuments appear to be built to remember the victims of our enemies and not of our victims."

"The Kayapo people of Amazonia call us the 'termite people' because we gobble up all that lives."

"A reporter in Australia asked me what I thought would be the ideal population for Australia? I answered – 'about a half a million…Aboriginals.'"
☠☠☠☠☠☠☠

☠☠☠☠☠☠☠

"After reading Dee Brown's book Bury My Heart at Wounded Knee, I headed down to South Dakota to volunteer as a medic for the American Indian Movement for the occupation of Wounded Knee and the establishment of the Independent Oglala Nation of Wounded Knee."

Ward Churchill in a debate at the Environmental Law School in Eugene, Oregon accused me of lying about my participation in the occupation of Wounded Knee.
"Our elders that I have spoken to say you were not there? Are you saying they are liars?"
My response: "No, I am not saying they are liars, I'm simply saying they are not telling the truth."
One thing I do know for sure was that Ward Churchill was not there in Wounded Knee during that time."

"A reporter in Australia asked me what I thought would be the ideal population for Australia? I answered – 'about a half a million…Aboriginals.'"

"Our ships fly the flag of the Six Nations given to us by the Mohawks. We fly the Aboriginal flag given to us by the Aboriginal people and we fly the Moari flag given to us by the Maori."

On Himself

"You don't get anywhere unless you've had a little bit of a complicated life."

☠☠☠☠☠☠☠

"I was raised in an Eastern Canadian fishing village. You could always spot the poor kids in this town. We were the ones who brought lobster sandwiches on homemade bread to school where we tried desperately to trade them for baloney or peanut butter on Wonder Bread."

"I had two pet lobsters when I was in first grade.
Flounderface and Bugeye. I set them free."

"I used to swim with a family of beavers in a beaver pond when I
was 10. I went back when I was 11 and found there were no more
beavers. I found that trappers had killed them all, so I became
quite angry and that winter
I began to walk the trap lines where
I would free the animals and destroy the traps."

"When I was a child, I almost drowned and at the time in my
mind I surrendered to the sea and accepted my fate. As it was, I
did not drown, but the result has been that I have never feared the
sea since, and it is the one place that I feel the safest and most
secure."

"When I think about it, I'm amazed I survived my childhood."

"The former Governor of Washington State, the late Dixie Lee
Ray once said that evidence of my insanity is that when I was a
boy of twelve, I shot another boy in the rear end with a bb gun
because he was about to shoot a bird. She said that any boy that
would should another boy to save a bird had to be insane. All I
can say is that in my hometown every boy shot every other boy
with a bb gun. I simply had a practical reason to shoot the boy
that I shot."

"I would say that nobody could do what I do unless you have a big ego. It's the only way you can really put it. You have to be arrogant enough to challenge the arrogance of the human race."

"I am not a captain by permission of some bureaucrat. I am a captain by virtue of passion and experience."

"You know, I wouldn't think I was successful if I don't have just as many people hate me as support me. You can't change things by not pissing people off."

"If I have to say just what it is I do best, I think my answer is that I'm good at delegating without micro-managing. If you ask me what the worst thing I do, I would say delegating without micromanaging."

I have been called a conservationist, a sea captain, an adventurer, a pirate, a historian, a writer, a teacher, a lecturer, a journalist, a terrorist and even worse a politician but the reality is that I have only been one thing and that is – a poet!

"Being a conservationist/environmentalist means saying things people don't want to hear, doing things that people don't like to see being done and pissing people off. It means rocking the boat, hell, it means sinking a few boats as well."

"I don't believe in retirement. The perfect job is one that you would do seven days a week, every day of the year for your entire life without pay. I love what I do."

☠☠☠☠☠☠

"The opinions of my critics have as much influence on me as a fart in a windstorm."

"I've never smoked anything in my life. It always seemed like a very unnatural thing to do."

"My greatest ambition is to eradicate the barbaric slaughter of whales, dolphins and seals."

"The most heroic thing that I never did was to rescue George Washington Hayduke in the Sea of Cortez."

"I look back on my time as a writer with the Georgia Straight as the 2nd most enjoyable and creative experience of my life. I mean it doesn't quite compare to sinking whaling ships and posing for pictures with penguins on the Ross Ice Shelf but I often feel I was born in the right time and fortunate enough to live in the right city to be a part of what was really the golden age of alternative journalism.'

"All that I could have ever wanted from life I have received: adventure, travel, the opportunity to save the lives of living things, romance, a beautiful intelligent wife, happiness, a wonderful daughter, an incredible son and two beautiful grandchildren. I am very content."

"Do I have any regrets?
Yes, but none that were really important".

"Have I made mistakes?
Plenty of them and everyone was a learning experience."

"When I was fifteen in 1964, I was stopped at the border when I
tried to enter Canada. The officer asked me where I was going.
"I'm heading to California to be a surfer."
Needless to say, I was refused entry."

☠☠☠☠☠☠☠

"During the Sixties and Seventies when hitching across Canada I found the best place to camp out was the cemeteries. No one bothers you in a cemetery."

"I've been married four times and divorced three times. Marriage ain't easy until you find the one that works."

"The lesson that being married four times is this: Don't commit unless you are 100% sure of your decision. Anything less than 100% will end in failure and unhappiness.'

"I can be forgiving up to a point but once that point is reached, there is no forgiveness. I shut the door on the relationship, I lock it and I toss the key into the sea."

"Jealousy is not in my character. Loyalty is present or it is not, and if not, I simply walk away."

"Experience has taught me that the secret to happiness is detachment from material desires, a focus on the desires of the heart and a curious mind, regardless of what people might think."

*"There is no rest on planetary duty.
The time to rest is in the grave."*

Inspiration

"Follow your dreams and use your natural-born talents and skills to make this a better world for tomorrow."

"I do what I do because it's the right thing to do. I am a warrior, and the way of the warrior to fight superior odds."

"In the great scheme of things, what matters is not how long you live but why you live, what you stand for and what you are willing to die for."

"Follow your dreams and use your natural-born talents and skills to make this a better world for tomorrow"

"I don't give a damn what any human on this planet thinks about us sinking whaling ships. We didn't sink those ships for humanity. We sank them for the whales.:

"I can't think of a more noble legacy then, "Because you lived, another species survived."

"A person who is mindful is a person free of stress."

"I'm not pessimistic about anything. You just have to have enough passion and perseverance. I always point out that in 1972, the very idea that Nelson Mandela would be president of South Africa was unthinkable, unimaginable and impossible. I'm eternally optimistic."

"In this struggle, there is no room for self-pity, and we cannot afford the luxury of pessimism. Courageous, imaginative and passionate people can turn the impossible into the possible. Those people are you, me and anyone who has the desire to change things."

"The pillars of life are built on the foundation of imagination, passion, courage and love. Our lives are strong only when these four cornerstones are strong. Remove one and we are incomplete. Remove two and we suffer depression, remove three and we begin to fade. Remove the fourth and we die!'

All the inspiration anyone needs is to watch the sun rise and the sun to set, to walk in the forest, to surf in the sea, to climb in the mountains, to sail, to dive, to snorkel, to hike and to explore. This planet offers everything we need to be inspired, to be happy and to be content.

Be Mindful of all the D's,
Your Dreams,
Your Desires,
Cherish Delight,
Cherish the Dawn.
Never Doubt Who You Are.
Avoid Depression,
Avoid Dementia,
Avoid Delirium,
Manage Destruction,
Dare to Live.
Accept the Inevitability of Death,
And Fulfil Your Destiny.

International Whaling Commission

"During the 1981 IWC meeting in Brighton, England I walked up to Juan Masso the owner of the two Spanish whaling ships we sank. I said:
"Hi, I would like to introduce myself, and as we shook hands I said, "I sank your ships you bastard."

"Sea Shepherd was banned from attending the annual meetings of the IWC in 1986. Three decades later we're still banned. That's what I call making a lasting impression."

"In 1997 with an invitation from Prince Alberta I attended the reception for the delegates to the IWC in Monaco. In response the delegations of Japan, Norway, Iceland and some of the Caribbean Islands I walked out in protest. I toasted them as they left saying to the Norwegians as they passed me, "when we can get Norwegians to walk out on free booze, that must mean we really pissed them off."

"In 1978 we opposed the whalers of Australia and it was a bitter fight. They did not surrender whaling without a struggle. That was over three decades in the past and today Australia is the strongest voice in the world in defense of the whales and that gives me hope that one day, Japan's voice will join in the same chorus."

☠☠☠☠☠☠☠

69

"Being banned from the IWC gave Sea Shepherd a real advantage. We did not have to pay the fees to attend and we had access to the media in the lobby of the hosting hotel. Being banned was an automatic guarantee of a media interview. Delegates and media would come to us and when we entered the restaurants, the Japanese and Norwegian delegates would walk out in protest. And Sea Shepherd was always a topic of debate thanks to Japan and Norway"

"The International Whaling Commission was set up by whaling nations for the whaling industry. Over a period of a decade whale conservationists were able to seize it from the whalers by achieving a global moratorium on commercial whaling. The problem of course was that the only enforcement powers lay with the signatory nations and none of them wanted to offend Japan."

"The IWC had the regulations without the authority to enforce the regulations so I decided that Sea Shepherd would take on the role of enforcing the IWC regulations which we proceeded to do with great enthusiasm."

"The IWC began in 1946. An organization that has always done too little too late and has been all talk and posturing without enforcement or credibility. With the election of Japanese whaling Commissioner Joji Morishita as chairman, the IWC has been effectively hijacked by pirate whalers."

The Law

"Sometimes you just need to break the law
before the law breaks you."

"My legal tips:
Nobody talks, everybody walks
Nobody signs, Everythings fine.
'Never admit nuthin'."

"Justice must always take precedence over the law."

"It was illegal under the laws of the democratically elected
government of Adolf Hitler to rescue Jews from the NAZI death
camps and that illustrates that sometimes you just have to break
some goddamn laws."

"In response to the criticism that Sea Shepherd walks a very fine
line when it comes to the law, I can only reply that it does not
matter how fine the line is
as long as the line is not crossed."

"All great social reformers and champions of noble causes have
experienced the insides of a jail cell.
That's just the way it is."

"I've been a guest of a few jails in my life. I've enjoyed the
hospitality of jails in Iran, Germany, the USA, Iceland and
Canada and I can say without reservation that the best damn jails
are in the Netherlands."

"I picked up a few good tips about quite a few things when I was
in prison. It was profoundly educational."

71

☠☠☠☠☠☠☠

*"What is the taxonomical definition of a lawyer?
The larval phase of a politician."*

"When the law breaks the law, there is no law."

*"In this movement it's hard to trust anyone who has never seen
the inside of a jail."*

*"Lawyers are like gun-fighters in the old west. When your life and
freedom depend upon having a lawyer, you need to get the best
damn gun in town, no matter the cost."*

"The law serves power, do not expect to be treated fairly."

*"It is always best to work within the boundaries of the law and
practicality when possible."*

Life and Death

*"The only people afraid of dying are people
who have never lived".*

*"You have not lived until you've
found something worth dying for."*

*"I don't think it is unusual to ask someone to risk their life to
defend a whale, it seems to me to be a more noble pursuit than to
risk one's life for a piece of cloth, someone else's real estate or
some corporation's oil well."*

"The meaning of life is life."

*"During the time that I served as a medic with the Oglala Lakota
at Wounded Knee, South Dakota in 1973, I learned two very
important lessons. The first is that we must do what we do without
any concern for winning or losing, victory or defeat but because it
is the right thing, the only thing we can do and the second thing is
the two Lakota words summing up why we go into battle and
those words are "hoka hey" meaning "It's a good day to die."*

"I used to believe in reincarnation but that was in my former life, not this one."

'Someone once asked me what song I would like played at my funeral? I don't really care because I won't be there."

"Life is a crazy dance with the graces where everyone ends up in the exact same place at the end, with most no wiser than when the dance began."

"Suicide is a permanent solution to a temporary problem."

☠☠☠☠☠☠☠

"The love of life inspires passion for life which motivates the passionate defense of life. And in a most ironic way, such passion for life allows the peaceful acceptance and understanding of the value your death has in the vibrant dance of the continuum."

"If it's ever reported that I committed suicide, I'll want an autopsy. I remember what happened to Abby Hoffman.

*"The one thing I know with absolute certainty
is that I will die.
The how, the when, and the where
are not really that important."*

"When I die, I think my epitaph should be: Good luck everyone, I hope you make it through this century."

LOVE

"My wife is the beacon of my life,
My son is my hope for the future.
She provides the light
to show me the way,
He is building the bridge to tomorrow,
Her light and his bridge
are my gifts every day."

"You can't force anyone to love you.
Nor can you force yourself to love someone.
Without a mutual connection there is nothing.
Nothing but resentment and bitterness."

"If you love someone, let them know.
The worst they can do in response is to say "no".
A "no" means walk away, it is not meant to be."

"You can't search for love. Love will find you when you where,
and when you least expect it."

"I have loved foolishly. I have loved seriously and sincerely. I
have loved passionately, romantically, and devoutly. But I have
also loved dishonestly, casually, flippantly and dispassionately.
The one absolute definition of love is that love is a complicated
series of lesson that shape the essence of our lives for better or
for worse."

Media and Movies

"I'm not a real pirate, I just play one on TV."

"The most powerful weapon in the world is the camera."

'We live in a media culture and whoever controls and influences and uses media the best has the power for change."

"The media is not concerned with facts, figures, statistics or scientific reports. The media is interested in drama, scandal, violence, celebrity and sex."

"We live in a media culture and media defines reality and this means that to get a message across we need to give the media what the media wants and usually that simply involves packaging, for what the media wants is the drama of sex, scandal, celebrity or violence. The more of these four elements that can be harnessed to a message, the more exposure the message will receive."

"There are four elements of media.
Sex, scandal, violence and celebrity.
Every story has to have one or more of these four elements.
If you have all four elements, you have a super story.
It does not matter what the truth is. The truth is irrelevant. The media will manufacture the truth and the truth is whatever the media wants people to believe."

"The camera is the most powerful weapon ever invented. If it was not captured on film, it didn't happen. That is the nature of media today"

☠☠☠☠☠☠☠

"Blood on the deck is a story."

"I don't manipulate the media. I did not make the rules. The media makes the rules and I play by their rules."

"When I hear so-called professional journalists ask why we resort to having celebrities speak for us and for the animals, the environment or social causes, I marvel at their denial of the rules of their own trade."

"That's this thing with celebrities: the media can't ignore them."

"Some people complain that I manipulate the media. Well, duh, we live in a media culture, so why on Earth wouldn't I."

"Being lampooned on 'South Park' is hardly something to complain about. They brought the issue of the dolphin and whale slaughter by the Japanese to a very large audience. I could not really care less how I was portrayed."

"The power of an idea can only be felt by the ability to transform that idea into action and thus an idea should be delivered like a bomb, more accurately a mind bomb, and detonated within the environment of mass media where it will touch the imagination and the sensitivities of millions."

"A book is a mind bomb. So is an article in a magazine, but film is the greatest mind bomb media there is with the power increasing ten-fold from documentary to television series to motion picture. Place your idea in a major motion picture or a television series and you can change the world."

"The best way to deal with trolls and unwanted critics can be summed up with two words; block & delete."

☠☠☠☠☠☠☠

"The internet is like the Bible, anything you want to find to justify
anything you want to do or back up any accusation you may wish
to make can be found written by someone for many reasons. What
the internet and especially Facebook has done has eliminated
editors and editors were once the guardians against
misinformation sneaking through
the doors into the public consciousness.
Today those doors are wide open.'

"I don't think that any government has a right to subvert the truth
or to cover up the truth, and all I see Wikileaks doing is exposing
the truth."

"Musicians and actors have made incredible contributions to the
conservation and environmental movement
and continue to do so."

"The best way to deal with trolls and unwanted critics can be
summed up with two words; block & delete."

Attending a lecture by Marshall McLuhan in the Seventies was
like sitting at the foot of Socrates or Plato. If ever there was a
guru of communications, McLuhan was it.

Although I detest the man, I have to agree that there is "fake
news". Not the kind that Trump is harping on about but the fact
that the news media is corporate controlled and reports only what
it decides to report on, based on the interests of sponsors and the
political views of the owners.

The media decides that a story is a story if it contain one or more of four basic elements - sex, scandal, violence and celebrity. A 4-element story is a super story.

*"I have made more money every year since 1981,
selling the rights to my life story than
I will ever make if a movie is actually made."*

*"A sequel to the Movie Groundhog Day would be easy to make.
They just need to re-release the same movie without changing a
thing and call it Groundhog Day II"*

*"The ten best movies that I have seen in my life are
(1) Lawrence of Arabia. (2) Das Boot. (3) The Treasure of Sierra
Madre. (4) Blade Runner. (5) Master and Commander. (6) Silent
Running. (7) The Last of the Mohicans. (8) Moby Dick. (9)
Twenty Thousand Leagues Under the Sea, (10) The Graduate."*

*"The ten best documentaries I have been in are (1) Sharkwater.
(2) Ocean Warriors. (3) Pirate for the Sea. (4) Eco-Pirate. (5)
The Cove. (6) (7) Why Just One? (8) How to Change the World.
(9) Battleship Antarctica.
(10) Watson. It's a biased list, I admit."*

*"Buck and the Preacher in 1972 was criticized for being
ridiculously politically correct for having two Black Cowboys.
What next, some people said – Black Vikings? The thing is there
were Black cowboys, plenty of them but Hollywood has
whitewashed them out of the movies Sidney Poitier and Harry
Belafonte were not being politically correct they were in fact
correcting history."*

The Ocean the Earth and Mars

If the Ocean dies, we all die!

'The reality is that this is not the planet Earth. It is the planet Ocean. The continents are islands in this one Ocean."

"I differentiate the sea from the Ocean. Many people think that the sea is the Ocean, however it is but one part of it, the part that is the most obvious.'

"The Ocean however is the entire planet and the one element that gives all living things the gift of life. It is water in continuous circulation, underground, in rivers and lakes, in the clouds, locked in glacial ice and coursing through the cells of every single living plant and animal."

"The truth is that each and every one of us is the Ocean, it is within us and it surrounds us, we are immersed in it and it flows through our bodies and into the ground, to the sea, transforming into gas and solids and back to liquid again and thus when we diminish any part, we diminish the whole and when we pollute any part of it, we pollute ourselves."

"The ocean, this great shroud of mystery is a blanket that cradles diversity and sustains life for all living things upon this planet."

"When plastic replaces fish, when we reach that point where there is more plastic in the sea than fish, there will be no turning back for humanity. We will effectively have committed collective suicide. "

☠☠☠☠☠☠☠

"Since 1950 we have seen a 40% diminishment in phytoplankton populations in the Ocean. Phytoplankton produces well over half the oxygen all animals need to breathe. Phytoplankton is diminished because whales, fish and sea-bird populations have been diminished. These animals, especially cetaceans provide the essential nutrients like iron and nitrogen to feed the phytoplankton. If phytoplankton disappear, humanity will be no more."

"Within the sea lies our darkest secrets, our greatest treasures, the greatest truths, our greatest mysteries and our only hope."

"The Ocean speaks, and we must listen!"

"The height of human ignorance is to say we need to save the planet. The planet does not need saving from us. The planet will survive. This is about saving humanity and thousands of other species from ourselves."

"Our Earth is a spaceship and we are on a voyage around this immense Milky Way galaxy, so immense that we have only circumnavigated the Galaxy twenty times during the history of the planet and the last time our planet was where it is now in relation to the Galaxy was some 250 million years ago which was the time of the great Permian extinction event when we lost some 97% of all life on the planet."

"What is truly amazing to me is that the Earth now has rings like Saturn and appropriately these rings are composed of urine and feces from thousands of space station dumps over the last few decades. Golden meteor showers anyone?

☠☠☠☠☠☠☠

"I have seen the photo taken from outside our solar system and it was wonderful to behold. All that we are, all that we have ever been and all that we will ever be resides on this tiny blue white dot against the immense blackness of space. The photo at once evokes our insignificance and at the same time expresses the essence of what we are – explorers fearlessly venturing into the infinite, undeterred by our insignificance in our search for significance."

"With the discovery of water on Mars, I felt immediately that there was a need to establish the Martian Conservation Society to defend possible Martians from human invasion."

People I've Known

FARLEY MOWAT

"The father I should have had, my friend, my mentor and my inspiration. In my mind, the greatest Canadian to have ever lived, a literary treasure to the nation who taught me that truth can be communicated best in fiction."

"I have known Farley Mowat all of my life, from reading his books as a child to becoming a close friend of his over the last three decades."

"Farley Mowat was, continues to be, and will for evermore be the true spirit of what a Canadian should be. A defender of nature and the First Nations, a profoundly talented storyteller, and a visionary who understood that Canada, our Canada is a nation of a million species and thus a repository of diversity that we as Canadians have a sacred responsibility and an obligation to honor and protect.

ALBERT FALCO

"Captain Albert Falco saw the diminishment of biodiversity in our oceans over a span of nearly seven decades. He was dedicated to the protection of life and habitats in the sea. He was a legendary mariner, diver, oceanographer, and conservationist. The world is a better place because of him."

ROBERT HUNTER

"Without Robert Hunter, Greenpeace would not exist today."

ROB STEWART

"Toronto filmmaker Rob Stewart was an aquatic guardian angel for the "demons" of the deep. "(Toronto Globe and Mail (Feb. 02/, 2017)

JET JOHNSON

"Fighter Pilot. 747 pilot. Founder of Greenpeace USA. The working girl's Errol Flynn."

PATRICK MOORE

"Patrick Moore is a corporate whore, an eco-Judas who betrayed everything he once stood for."

MARGARET MEAD
BUCKMINSTER FULLER

"Margaret Mead and Buckminster Fuller were the first two members of the Sea Shepherd Advisory Board. They lent us their vision and their dreams."

PETER HELLER

"Peter Heller wrote a book about Sea Shepherd in Antarctica about our Southern Ocean crew and called it Ocean Warriors. The poseur Pete Bethune simply high-jacked that title and removed the 's"
declaring himself, as 'the' Ocean Warrior."

CLEVELAND AMORY

"Cleveland Amory, the kindest, gentlest, grumpiest and most compassionate curmudgeon I've ever met."

BOB GELDOF

*"Many of the people I worked with at the Georgia Straight moved
on to become rather famous in a diversity of ways. I remember in
1975, having a beer in the Anchor with Bob Geldof. He was
heading back to London to form a band. "You have got to be
kidding, Bob, you can't even sing."*

DOUG TOMKINS

*"Doug Tomkins transformed
clothing into wilderness preservation.
He lived and he died for wilderness preservation. "*

SYLVIA EARLE

*"A woman of spectacular depth of insight
into the mysteries of the sea."*

EDWARD ABBEY

*"I will forever be grateful for Abbey recruiting me into the
Monkey Wrench Gang."*

WALRUS OAKENBOUGH

*"We fought at Wounded Knee together, we fought for the wolves
in the Peace River together and we sailed forth to challenge
Soviet whalers together. David Garrick my brother is probably
the closet person that I have ever known that I would call a truly
mindful warrior monk and saint. "*

BRIGITTE BARDOT

"Inside this remarkable woman is a heart of fierce compassion. I have seen her strength and resolve on the bucking ice floes off Labrador and I am proud that for over four decades she has been, a true and loyal friend. "

STERLING HAYDEN

"What most impressed me about Hayden was the aura of self-confidence and contentment he wore, making him look like he was born in the weathered pea coat he was wearing, like he was a man who knew who he was, where he was going, and what was important in life."

MARTIN SHEEN

"One of the most compassionate, caring and most Catholic men that I have ever had the pleasure of knowing and working with. He's an activist who happens to be an actor and should have been the real President of the United States instead of playing the role on television."

RUSSELL MEANS

"Russell taught me the art of confrontation. Ignore the odds and don't be concerned about winning or losing. Act because it is the right thing to do, the right time and the right place to do it. Our actions in the present will define the future."

Pirates

"Pirates get things done."

"Pirate ships were the cradles of democracy. Captains were elected and color was not a barrier to advancement and this was in the 17th century."

"If you want to stop piracy, you need a pirate to do so. Henry Morgan succeeded where the Royal Navy failed."

"The founder of the United States Navy, John Paul Jones, was a pirate."

"The first democracies on ships, where race and gender were not obstacles to promotion, where a fierce code of honor prevailed and freedom was respected above all else. Pirates were robbers who stole gold from thieves."

"The real pirates off Somalia are the foreign fishing fleets that raped clean the Somali waters of life and drove fishermen into abject impoverished desperation."

"Sea Shepherd is a Navy or compassionate pirates in pursuit of ecologically destructive pirates driven by greed"

"U.S. Federal 9th Circuit Court Judge Alex Kozinski officially designated me as a bona fide pirate, something for which I am deeply honored."

Politics

*"I choose to be ecologically correct
rather than politically correct."*

*"My politics have always been Green and will always be Green.
Not on the Left, not on the Right but planted in the soil, on the sea
or in the trees."*

*"The Sea Shepherd Conservation Society is a conservative
organization. I am a conservative. You can't get more
conservative than being a conservationist. Our entire raison de
etre is to conserve and protect. The radicals of the world are
destroying our oceans and our forests, our wildlife and our
freedom."*

*"I once ran for Mayor of Vancouver in order to use the mayoral
race as a platform to address environmental issues. There was
one frightening moment when I realized that I actually had a
chance of winning.
Winning was definitely not my objective.'*

*"It's difficult to vote when your only two choices are a
Republicrat or a Demopublican."*

*"I can name the politicians that I trust on one hand. Elizabeth
May (Green Party) of Canada. Bob Brown and Peter Whish-
Wilson of Australia (Green Party). Nicolas Hulot of France
(Environment Minister) and Tulsi Gabbard of the USA.
(Congresswoman for Hawaii."*

☠☠☠☠☠☠☠

"People are sheep.
April 15th is the day the sheep get sheared".

"The Palestinians are the Indians of the Middle East. Their land stolen by invaders, persecuted and subjected to genocidal polices of an occupying government."

"In my travels around the world I have found the one thing that almost all politicians have in common is corruption. There are exceptions, but such exceptions are very rare."

"I don't look on countries as countries. I don't recognize countries. To me they are just abstractions that divide people. The planet doesn't have lines on it, you know. Back a few years ago I went to a restaurant in the US called Medieval Times. You go there and watch knights on horseback. They are jousting and you get a medieval meal. It's really an insight into nationalism because you don't have any choice where you sit just like you don't have any choice where you're born. They sat us in the blue section – there's also the red section, black section, yellow section, etc. – and you get to cheer for your knight. The blue knight. Which is fine. It's fun. Except twenty minutes later the blue section hates the yellow section. The red section hates the black section. 'Leave our knight alone!' people shout. It's a completely fabricated thing. It means absolutely nothing. The same thing is true with nationalism. It's taking sides. It's like tribalism, really. There is no difference among people."

Religion

"I once believed in reincarnation but that was in my previous life, not this one."

"Religion is simply the insanity of humanity, a form of collective psychosis."

"You don't see many atheist suicide bombers. Not much of a future in it."

"When people ask me how creation could happen without a God, my response is how did God happen without creation?"

"If Jesus was born from a virgin, he could not have had a Y chromosome therefore he had to be a she or at the very least trans-gender."

"Any religion that places humans at the center of creation is a fantasy. Humans have never been, are not and will never be the center of creation. We are just one of millions of species and we have not even been around that long. We just believe we have."

?The Bible says that Methuselah lived to be 926 years of age. He actually only lived to age 77. In other words he lived for 926 moons because that was how time was measured a few thousand years ago."

"The entire foundation of the Catholic Church was built around a vision by St. Paul as a result of ingesting moldy rye. Ergot is the mold on rye and ergot is the natural origin of LSD. Paul was high when he spoke to God."

94

☠☠☠☠☠☠☠

"I've been working on a book now for twenty years about the history of Christianity. The title is God's Monkey House. I had a chapter called All the Dope on the Popes. There was so much dope on the popes that the chapter became a book in itself."

"Religion is simply a form of collective mass psychosis."

"If God is so powerful, so mighty and omnipotent, why does he always need money?"

"If God has something to say to me, he can bloody well say it to my face. I don't trust his spokespeople."

"As Pope Leo X once said: "This myth of Christ has served us well."

"Jews murdering chickens in the streets of New York, Muslims slitting the throats of sheep in the streets of Cairo, Christians tossing goats off the steeple of churches, they can call it religion, but I'll call it sadistic perversion."

"I have no respect for any religion that views humans as superior to other animals."

"If people can believe in Mormonism and Scientology, they can believe in absolutely anything."

"I was forced to read the Bible as a child, so many damn times I practically memorized it and I found it to be the most offensive, violent, racist, sexist piece of wasted pulp that I have ever read. I do however appreciate the church for making me read this book. It was very educational but not in the manner they had in mind."

☠☠☠☠☠☠☠

"How many Christian gods are there?
Aside from Jehovah, there is Samuel a.k.a. Satan,
Plus, the Archangels, the Cherubs, the Principalities and their
millions of retainers. In fact there are more Gods (immortals) in
Christianity than there are in Hinduism."

"If there is a hell which I am 100% sure there is not, it will be
much nicer than this reality is for animals. To non-humans, this is
hell and we are the demons."

"All three Abrahamic religions emerged from a small little circle
in the Middle East. The rest of the world did not choose to follow
Abraham, Jesus and Mohammed. The sword and the cannon had
a great deal to do with the spread of these ideas and an ocean of
blood was spilt to advance the propaganda. Our entire world
would be a kinder, gentler, more aware, more mindful and more
peaceful place if these three seeds from God's Monkey House had
been contained within that silly little circle of delusional and
violent men."

"I find it fascinating that all the characters in the Old testament are non-White people and the only White people in the New Testament are the Romans who persecuted Jesus Christ. And yet all the pictures that I see of Jesus have blondish hair and blue eyes. I sense a modicum of deception and hypocrisy here."

"I believe I will create a new religion – the Church of Biocentrism. A religion that places us as part of the biosphere and not lord and master over it, a religion that believes in equality amongst all species and respect for all species, a religion that promotes harmony amongst all species and a religion that appreciates the continuum of life."

Ships

I am the commander of Neptune's Navy

Ships are expendable, whales are not.

The only thing scarier than Godzilla is Godzilla's lawyers (In response to the Japanese lawyers saying we could not name a ship Gojira.)

I named our fast trimaran the Gojira because I wanted to see the headline in the Japanese newspaper stating: Gojira Attacks Whaling Fleet.

We changed the name of the Gojira to the Brigitte Bardot, thus turning the beast into the beauty.

To experience what it's like to be a ship owner, picture yourself standing in a cold shower dropping $100-dollar bills down the drain endlessly.

Not a single person has ever been killed or injured on any ship under my command.

With ships, it is always something and if it's not something, it's something else, but it is always something.

Our ships proudly fly the flag of the Iroquois Confederacy that was given to us by the Mohawks in 2007.

☠☠☠☠☠☠☠

"The future hides in the fog, the present endures, but at these times I let the wind set the course, knowing that the ship will carry on as it may."

"I first crossed the equator in 1969 onboard a Norwegian freighter. I first circumnavigated the world in 1972. My first transit of the Panama Canal was in 1981. The furthest North that I have sailed in the Bering Strait in 1981 and the furthest South was the Bay of Whales in 2011."

"My first typhoon was in the South China Sea in 1969. I thoroughly enjoyed it. I read Conrad's Typhoon with a glass of wine with ambience."

"As a boy of six, sitting at the end of the dock in St. Andrews- -By-the-Sea overlooking the Passamaquoddy Bay I knew that my destiny would be the sea."

Sierra Club

*"Being a national director of the Sierra Club was enlightening.
I called it the Siesta Club Conversation Society."*

*"When I became a Sierra Club National Director (2003-2006) I
thought I was going to be a director of a conservation society.
Instead I found that we were just a wing of the Democratic
Party."*

*"I resigned from the Sierra Club when they sponsored a: 'Why I
like to Hunt Essay Contest'
I told them it was disrespectful of the Sierra Club Founder John
Muir, who had called hunting – the 'murder business.'"*

*'At a quarterly meeting in Albuquerque, New Mexico, Executive
Director Carl Pope brought in some folks from the inner cities to
lecture the 15 directors on our priorities, that we should focus on
poverty and social justice issues.
I said: "I joined the Sierra Club because of my concern for
forests, wildlife, wetlands and nature, not for people. Of every
charitable dollar, 99 cents goes to people and only 1 cent goes to
environmental causes. People need to keep their greedy paws off
our penny.
One of the intercity men called me a racist for saying that.
I responded: Don't you call me a racist. I'm a misanthrope. I
dislike everyone equally."*

☠☠☠☠☠☠☠

"There were two Important things the Sierra Club absolutely refused to discuss. The first was human population and immigration issues and the 2nd was the impact of eating meat on the environment."

"I knew that my membership with the Sierra Club was over when I spent hours in a Board meeting debating the issue of removing the ethical filters from their 'investment portfolio."

"One director said, "we have a fiduciary responsibility to invest donor money for the best return financially. I replied, "We have no such thing, we have an ethical responsibility to invest their money, defending nature and the damn planet."

"During my three years with the Sierra Club I felt like I was part of an elite Gourmet Club. It was Buffalo steak in Montana, Blue crabs in Charleston, Lobster in Boston and each and every meal there was always the same old Portobello mushroom meal for us silly vegans along with a lecture that veganism was unhealthy."

'For daring to speak to the L.A. Times as a Sierra Club Director on the issue of population I was officially admonished by the Board. I attended the next meeting wearing a T-shirt I had made emblazoned with yellow letters on black saying "admonished" They were not amused."

Travel

"There are travelers and there are tourists. I've never understood tourism. Tourists always seem to be seeking the comforts and familiarity of home when they travel. They see things without experiencing the things they see."

"I shipped out to sea at seventeen to places only seamen have seen and had experiences that shaped the rest of my life."

"At 18, I experienced apartheid in South Africa, survived a bar fight in Beira, Mozambique, had drinks with FRELIMO revolutionaries in the jungle outside of Laurenco Marques, spent a week with a Zulu girl on the beach, saw my first wild lion, my first wild elephant and discovered real quick how ridiculously fast a crocodile can run."

"At 21, I was busted for espionage in Iran. They thought I was a British spy because it said British subject in my passport. They did not know where Canada was, but the best-selling soda in the country was Canada Dry ginger ale so I pointed to the map of Canada on the bottle and slowly said Canada until they seemed to understand that I was not actually British but was somehow connected to the bottle of ginger ale in some mysterious way."

"At 22, I lived on a beach on the island of Rhodes for six months trying to be a poet until I realized I did not have the life experience yet to actually be a poet."

✖✖✖✖✖✖✖

"In 1972, I travelled around the world in eighty days on eighty cents. Now that was one hell of an adventure.
In 1973, I was banned for life from the Parthenon for making love with a Japanese woman in the Temple of Aphrodite. I argued that what was the point of a Temple for Aphrodite without sex? Six months later I was banned for life a second time for climbing the Parthenon to photograph the hidden steel girders holding up the place."

"I was a tour guide in Turkey and Syria in 1974, taking groups of western women on two-week bus tours from Istanbul to Aleppo and back. It was always amusing with each new group trying to explain how to use Turkish toilets. The looks on their faces was priceless."

"During my travels I always tried to avoid anyone sporting a Canadian flag on their pack or clothing. If I wanted to spend times talking with Canadians, I would have stayed home."

Veganism

"Nobody can legitimately claim to be a marine ecologist and conservationist while continuing to eat fish. It is hypocrisy."

"Atlantic puffins starve to death so that Danish factory farmed chickens can consume their fish."

"A Vegan driving a Hummer contributes less greenhouse gases to the atmosphere than a meat eater riding a bicycle."

"Humans are not and never have been carnivores like lions, tigers and wolves, we're more like vultures, jackals and flies - eaters of dead meat. A more appropriate word would be 'necrovore.'"

"I do not like proselytizing by anyone and that includes veggie-Jesuits. Veganism should be practiced, not preached."

"Sea Shepherd ships began as vegetarian ships in 1979 and became 100% vegan vessels beginning in 1999."

"The meat industry produces more greenhouse gases than the entire transportation industry."

"Sixty-five billion animal lives snuffed out each year plus the billions of fish murdered in the sea, baby chicks ground up in machines, baby cows taken from their mothers and enclosed in dark isolated boxes, animals suffering from thirst, from abuse, from neglect, starved, beaten and slaughtered without compassion. This is a horrific on-going holocaust and an indictment on the inhumanity of humanity.
You really can't be a credible environmentalist if you consume products from the animal agriculture industry."

Whale Wars

"Attention all crew, stand by to ram."

"People sometimes feel frustrated about what's going on in our oceans and environment, and 'Whale Wars' demonstrates that ordinary people can take action to make things happen."

"It is true that many of the Sea Shepherd crewmembers are inexperienced, but the fact is that these volunteers bring a passion to the project that cannot be found in a hired crew."

"In 'Deadliest Catch,' we have men in ships in rough cold seas doing dangerous things in a very remote area for the purpose of catching crabs. I said to Animal Planet that I could give them men and women from many nations working in a colder, much rougher and more remote ocean doing something far more dangerous for the purpose of saving whales. Plus, we could throw in some penguins, orcas and icebergs. That's how I sold them on Whale Wars."

"Animal planet did not tell us what to do or where to go and we did not tell them what to shoot or how to edit the show. We did not have a script. We did what we did as if they were not there and they followed with their cameras."

Writing and Poetry

"Poets are the manipulators of words and rhyme
Seeking to express the inexpressible urges
Charting the flow of our passions through time
From elated rejoicing to mournful dirges."

"On the ragged edge of the world I'll roam,
And the home of the whale shall be my home,
And saving seals on the remote ice and snows,
The end of my voyage... who knows, who knows?"

"I have no concerns for the media spin,
At the lies and falsehoods, they scatter.
May the future forgive my ecological sin,
For all other sins don't matter."

"To be a good writer, open up your heart and soul, unleash your
imagination and give free rein to your intuition."

"A real poem writes itself. When I start a poem, I have no idea
where and when it will end."

"The greatest compliment that I have ever received is that
Leonard Cohen liked my poems."

"I have been many things in my life. Master mariner,
conservationist, teacher, adventurer, author and lecturer. But the
one thing to me that has mattered the most is being a poet."

Captain Watson's Most Controversial Quotes

"Yes, the deaths of four sealers is a tragedy but the slaughter of hundreds of thousands of seal pups is an even greater tragedy." (When asked to apologize on live TV, I smiled and said, "I apologize --- for being a Canadian and associated with this cruel and barbaric industry.")

"Earthworms are far more valuable than people."
The folks on FOX TV went ballistic over this comment. I was asked to apologize for this. I replied, "I can't apologize for stating what is an ecological truth."

"If you don't know an answer, a fact, a statistic – make it up on the spot.
This statement is in my book Earthforce! It was taken out of context by my critics. In the book I was referring to President Ronald Reagan's method of speaking with the media.

"There's nothing wrong with being a terrorist, as long as you win. Then you write the history."
A favorite of my critics. This quote was taken out of context. I was citing a fact of history that terrorism was practiced by Israel, by American and French revolutionaries and when these terrorists won, they were considered heroes and not terrorists.

Exchanges

CANADIAN PRIME MINISTER
PIERRE TRUDEAU

In 1977 Prime Minister Pierre Elliott Trudeau and I had a short debate on the lawn at the University of California in Berkley. I was there to confront him on the seal slaughter in Canada. Prime Minister Trudeau: "If you're opposed to killing seals for fur, why are you wearing leather shoes?"

I looked at my bare feet and back at the Prime Minister: "I suppose they are leather."

He was not amused.

☠☠☠☠☠☠☠

CANADIAN PRIME MINISTER
JUSTIN TRUDEAU AND MARGARET TRUDEAU

I first met Justin Trudeau in 1972. I had gone to school (Simon Fraser University) with his mother Margaret Sinclair. I ran into her in front of the Hotel Vancouver. He was a cute little baby in a stroller. I said to her, "Maybe he will be Prime Minister someday."
She answered with a laugh, "I hope not."

☠☠☠☠☠☠☠

NEWFOUNDLAND
PREMIER BRIAN PECKFORD

I debated the Premier at Memorial University in St. John's
Newfoundland which was akin to Churchill agreeing to debate
Hitler in Berlin in 1939. To stress that I was not an outsider, I
began by saying I was an
eighth generation Maritimer.

Peckford responded by saying, "so you're an eight generation
Marintime are ya Paul?
Well I'm a ninth generation Newfoundlander
so, what do you think of them apples, b'ye?"

"Jesus, Brian, I did not think this was a pissing conference."

☠☠☠☠☠☠☠

NEWFOUNDLAND
PREMIER DANNY WILLIAMS

"Former Newfoundland Premier Danny Williams made the silly
statement that Paul Watson is not welcome in Canada and
Newfoundland because he is a "terrorist." Captain Watson
simply laughed and said as a Canadian he was free to go to
Newfoundland when he wished, and that Danny Williams should
arrest him if he is a terrorist and stop talking about it if he is not.'

☠☠☠☠☠☠☠

LARS ULLRICH

*I was visiting with Sean Penn at his home in Northern California
in 2005. His neighbor came to visit, and Sean said, this is my
neighbor Lars.*
"Hi Lars," I said. "what do you do?"
"I play drums, I'm a musician." He said.
"Do you have a group," I asked.
"Yes," he said. "Metallica."
*"Oh, never heard of Metallica,
how are you doing?"*
He looked very surprised.
"You've never heard of Metallica?"
I thought for a moment,
*"Right, yes I have. Beavis and Butthead.
I think one of those guys wears your shirt."*

☠☠☠☠☠☠☠

JEAN MICHELLE COUSTEAU

*I was in Magdalena Bay, Mexico opposing the Mitsubishi salt
mining operations and I did not have a permit. A RIB approached
my RIB and onboard was Jean Michelle Cousteau. He seemed
upset that I was there and demanded to see my permit. I could not
resist: "Permit, I don't need no stinking permit." However, I
don't think he had seen the movie because he looked confused.*

☠☠☠☠☠☠☠

JOHN FRIZEL OF GREENPEACE

*After we sank half of Iceland's whaling fleet in 1986, I ran into
John Frizell of Greenpeace.
John gave me a missionary-like look of disapproval
when he saw me.
"You know Watson, all of us in Greenpeace think that what you
did in Iceland is despicable, criminal, and unforgivable."
"And your point is John?" I asked.
"I thought you should know what we think. Your actions have
embarrassed this whole movement, you arrogant bastard."
"So?"
"You really don't care, do you?"
"No I don't John. We did not sink those whalers for Greenpeace
or for you, or for the movement, or for any human being on this
planet John. We sank them for the whales John. The whales, not
you, and frankly I could not give a damn what you, or anyone else
thinks. Find me a whale that disagrees with what we have done
and maybe I might give your opinion some thought.*

HARVEY WEINSTEIN

*At the Cannes Film Festival at a party on Queen Noor of
Jordans' yacht I approached Harvey Weinstein to introduce
myself. As I held out my hand and began to address him, he very
rudely said, "Fuck off asshole, you're blocking my view of Naomi
Watts." (A few years later, I was thrilled to see that the women he
assaulted took him down)*

113

ORSON WELLES

In the mid-Eighties I was visiting Maurice Seiderman, a friend of a friend in Port Angeles, Washington. I was sitting in his study alone when the phone rang.
Caller: "Hello, is Maurice there.
Me: "Not at the moment."
Caller: "I see, well tell him that Orson called."
Me: "Ok, Orson who?"
Caller: "Orson Welles, you idiot."
He hung up.

I had not been aware that Maurice Seiderman was a close friend of Orson Welles. Strangely I felt somewhat honored to have been called an idiot by Citizen Kane and the doomsday preacher from Moby Dick.

SIERRA CLUB EXECUTIVE - DIRECTOR CARL POPE

At the Telluride Film Festival in 2002 I was on a panel with Carl Pope who made no secret that he disliked me, which was okay because I did not like him much either.
A question from the audience was:
"What can one person do to defend the environment?"
Carl answered: "Talk to your neighbor. If everyone talked with their neighbor, we can save the environment."
I looked at him and said:
"Am I up here with freaking Mr. Rogers?"
The next year I was elected to the Sierra Club National Board of Directors. He was not happy.

A GERMAN BEAR HUNTER IN TOFINO

In 1993 when I brought our ship the Edward Abbey into Tofino, British Columbia I was doing an interview with a TV reporter about saving the forests, when a bear hunter about 60 years old with a thick German accent stormed up to me and told me to go, 'back where you came from."

I responded to me by asking him, "how many Jews did you kill in the war?"

The reporter was shocked. I repeated the words, "how many Jews did you kill in the war?"

"I was never in the war," he stammered.

"Yes, you were, I said, "you were in the war and you were a member of the SS."

The reporter said, "you can't accuse a man of being a war criminal just because he has a German accent."

"No," I answered. "Not because of his accent but because of his right hand. He's missing his trigger finger which meant because of his age and his accent, he was in the SS. The Russians removed the trigger finger of any SS soldiers they took prisoner, except the officers. They shot the officers in the head."

I looked at him, "are you denying you were a soldier with the SS? So I repeat, how many Jews did you kill in the war?

He angrily stormed off. I turned to the reporter, "now where were we?"

THE FBI

I was invited to speak on the topic of Sea Shepherd and activism to the FBI at FBI headquarters in Quantico, Virginia. It was an interesting event. During question and answer, an FBI special agent said to me that Sea Shepherd is walking a very fine line when it comes to the law. I replied that, "Does it matter how fine the line is if we don't actually cross the line?"
Another special agent said that we were training eco-terrorists. I asked him what he was referring to. He said that one of our volunteer crew had been sent to prison for crimes against property, for releasing mink from mink farms. I replied that I can't be responsible for what individuals do once they are no longer working with Sea Shepherd. He said, "you trained him so that makes you responsible. I replied, "I have three names for you. Timothy McVeigh, Lee Harvey Oswald, Osama Bin Laden. You trained them, does that make you responsible for their crimes?"

☠☠☠☠☠☠☠

THE CANADIAN COAST GUARD

During the sealing season in Canada's Gulf of St. Lawrence a Canadian Coast Guard captain called me on the VHF radio to ask what we were doing. I replied, "I am not in violation of any law, we have the right of free passage. But tell me, what are you doing here?"
He replied, "we are here to protect the sealers from the likes of you Mr. Watson."
I said to him, "Are you not here to protect the seals from the sealers as well?"
"No sir," He answered. "I believe that's your job."
I replied, "Well thank you for acknowledging that sir."

116

VERMONT STATE TROOPER (1967)

*I was hitchhiking through Northern Vermont in 1967 when a
Vermont State trooper pulled up and questioned me.
"Where ya from kid?"
I answered, "I'm from Canada."
He looked at me suspiciously. "You speak pretty good English for
a Canadian. Do you have any identification?"
I handed him my birth certificate.
He looked at me again even more suspiciously. "You said you
were from Canada, but it says here you're from Ontario."*

SOUTH AFRICAN SHIP INSPECTOR

*Upon arrival in Capetown on January 25th, 2006, our ship
Farley Mowat was boarded by Captain Saleem Modak of the
South African Maritime Safety Authority (SAMSA). He demanded
to see our registration and then informed me that the registration
was not valid because in his opinion our ship was not a yacht
although the registration papers were for a Canadian registered
yacht.
Captain Modak: "This ship is not a yacht. It is black and too
large to be a yacht; a yacht is a white ship where wealthy people
can sit and have drinks on the deck."
Myself: "Really I'm surprised. I would have thought that in post-
Apartheid South Africa there
would be room for a black yacht."*

CANADIAN BORDER GUARDS

*In 2008 I drove from Friday Harbor, Washington to attend the
funeral of one of my fellow Greenpeace co-founders, Dr. Lyle
Thurston. I drove up to the border guard and handed him my
Canadian passport.*

Officer : "How long do you intend to stay in Canada sir?"

Myself: "Does it matter?"

Officer : "What is your business in Canada sir?"

Myself: "Well quite frankly it's none of your business."

He directed me to go inside for further questioning.

2nd Officer: "Why you refuse to answer questions."

*Myself: "I don't have to answer stupid questions. I'm a Canadian
citizen and I do not have to tell you how long I will here or what
my business is in coming to my own country."*

*2nd Officer : "We can deny you entry if you don't answer our
questions."*

Myself: "Fine, deny me entry."

*2ndOfficer: "Sir, we can legally deny you entry. You have to
answer our questions."*

*Myself: "No I don't, so deny me entry so I can go to the media
with the story that a Canadian citizen was denied entry for
refusing to state his business in his own country."*

*2nd Officer: (becoming agitated). "Sir we're going to search your
car, is there anything there that should not be there?"*

Myself: "No, unless you plant something."

*Ten minutes later he came back looking somewhat disappointed
and said:*

"Sir do you have any outstanding warrants?"

I smiled: "Hell, I don't know, maybe you should check."

*I then said, "look you have a nice bench there and I have a good
book so I'm going to go sit on that bench and I'm going to read
my book and when you're finished with this bullshit, let me know,
ok?*

A few minutes later I was on my way to Lyle's funeral.

☠☠☠☠☠☠☠

SOVIET SOLDIER IN SIBERIA

*In August 1981, I landed on the beach at Lorino in Soviet Siberia
to get evidence on illegal whaling. There were two Soviet soldiers
patrolling the shore. They ignored us for about 45 minutes as we
documented the whaling station assuming we must be Russian
scientists. Returning to our RIB, one soldier walked up and
pointed at the boat.*
"Sto eta?" he said. (What is it).
"Eta Zodiac," I replied.
*"Nyet, eta Mercury," pointing now at the outboard motor.
I quickly turned my back on him and began to push the boat into
the water speaking softly to my two crew, "what is he doing?"*
"He's taking his rifle off his shoulder."
"Quickly," I said, "smile and wave."
*They did so and he turned and ran up the hill towards the town
and we got away.*

☠☠☠☠☠☠☠

119

SHOWDOWN WITH THE SOVIET NAVY

With our evidence in hand and having escaped the Soviet soldier on the beach, we returned to our ship and began to cruise down the coast of Siberia.

About an hour later to Soviet helicopter gunships buzzed by and began to shoot flares across our bow. I ignored them.

About 40 minutes later a large Soviet frigate approached and began to run alongside us. I ignored them also.

Suddenly the VHF radio crackled and a loud heavily accented voice said in English:

"Sea Shepherd, stop your ship and be prepared to be boarded by the Soviet Union."

I replied: "I am not stopping my ship. We don't have room for the Soviet Union."

We kept going and escaped back into U.S. waters

☠☠☠☠☠☠☠

In High School I had to play football. I played left tackle. I was not a big fan of football but playing was not voluntary. I did not really like it but I did learn a few valuable life lessons. One of those lessons was on how to deal with critics.

Some of the team were upset because some of the fans in the stands were calling them names.

The coach said that we just simply needed to ignore them. "They are spectators. You are players. They are watching you. You are not watching them nor should you, nor should you listen to them. Your focus needs to be on the opposing team. They are all that matters, they are the only thing that matters. All your energies must be directed at stopping the opposition on the field. Only they have the ability to defeat us. The spectators in the stands have no influence over us, no power over us - they are simply irrelevant, now get out there and secure some ground."

After that I never again looked to the stands – only to the field.

The End

Printed in Great Britain
by Amazon